The
Improv Mindset

CHANGE YOUR BRAIN.
CHANGE YOUR BUSINESS.

Bruce T. Montgomery
and
Gail Montgomery

John -
Enjoy!
Gail
~ Bruce

ExperienceYes Press
Evergreen, CO

D1360249

ExperienceYes Press
6551 Arapahoe Drive
Evergreen, CO 80439
www.experienceyes.com

Book Layout: BookDesignTemplates.com
Cover Design: Bruce & Gail Montgomery, inspired by Erin Wright (Asylum)

Ordering Information:
Quantity sales. Special discounts are available on quantity purchases by corporations, associations, and others. For details, contact the "Special Sales Department" at the address above.

The Improv Mindset / Montgomery & Montgomery. —1st ed.
ISBN 978-0-578-63575-0

ACKNOWLEDGEMENTS

We are deeply indebted to our clients and colleagues who encouraged us to write this book. Those people include: Wende & Brent Abrahm, Cristina Amigoni, Arthur Blume, Steve Brown, Meme Callnin, Jeff Carson, Alan Cohen, Linda Gallup, John & Jenn Langhus, Tom Miller, Dan Park, Travis Parkinson, Brian Peters, Josh Pinkert, Sarah Schillereff, Larry Siegel, Sara Steen, and the faculty of the Daniels College of Business at the University of Denver (including Charlie Knight, Barb Kreisman, Scott McLagan, and Kerry Plemmons).

We realize that we could not have gotten where we are without the support and sacrifices of our families. We are thankful for Peter & Betsy Montgomery, Jack Schnepp, Terri Schnepp, Cynthia Barclay, Steve Davis, Jack Montgomery, Paige Montgomery, David & Steffani Montgomery and Erin & Laura Wright.

"*I was blown away by how ExperienceYes unlocked my team's creative power. We are a team of highly creative people. Still, to see the idea generation of our team at DaVita go up by 41% was just astounding, and I can see the value of using these skills and tactics in future innovation sessions.*"

– Bill Myers, Vice President, Marketing, Communications & Corporate Social Responsibility, DaVita

"*We had a phenomenal experience with ExperienceYes from beginning to end, starting with the in-depth research they did to learn about and understand my organization and colleagues. From researching our business, to several in-person sessions discussing everything from personality types, leadership styles, challenges, and group dynamics, it was as if they were part of my team before they even arrived. I am excited to work with ExperienceYes moving forward in my hospital teams in many capacities. I cannot provide a stronger recommendation that you make them a part of your organization.*"

– Sarah Schillereff, DVM, Regional Vice President, VCA

"ExperienceYes takes leadership development to the next level. The facilitators encourage both personal and team growth at the same time. It was an extraordinary and innovative way for our Children's Hospital Colorado executive leaders to learn, grow...and laugh!"

– Nita Mosby Henry, Ph.D., Senior Vice President, HR, Children's Hospital Colorado

"We thought ExperienceYes was PHENOMENAL!!! Truly. You guys have definitely found your calling and what you offer people/organizations is so important and so great. Thank you for leading our team through your process! I hope to work with you again in the future.

– Kate Sparks, Program Developer, Executive Education, Daniels School of Business, University of Denver

"The Oil & Gas Industry is often a volatile and unpredictable industry. At Noble Energy, we strive to embrace creative thinking to make us flexible and agile. Bringing in ExperienceYes for our facility redesign project helped us to break down our existing thinking and get out of the "box" in which we were stuck. With their guidance, our team collaborated, innovated, and delivered solid results. We couldn't have gotten there without them."

– Brian Peters, Director – Major Projects, Noble Energy

"Kind of scary but fun and freeing! Gail and Bruce infused a new energy into the day (and week). I'm intrigued by how improv can translate into teamwork, better communication, and increased creativity in the workplace."

– Rocky Mountain Leadership Participant

MORE PRAISE FOR THE BOOK

"The Improv Mindset practices what it preaches by taking an innovative approach to increasing innovation. With their 30 years of experience in acting and in business, Bruce and Gail Montgomery demonstrate how unleashing the power of improvisational acting can help people generate more ideas, teams work together more effectively, and companies compete better. Every company and every person who wants to be more creative, more innovative, and more successful will benefit from the tools and techniques in this book."

– Daniel Park, Chief Campus Counsel, UC San Diego

"The Montgomery team put science and art together in a tidy package called The Improv Mindset. It is fascinating to see how understanding the neuroscience behind the creative process will help all of us get better at the innovation process. This book will be useful to our Executive MBA students as they combine the disciplines of finance, accounting, marketing, and leadership to build the organizations of the future. This is a great book for anyone looking to find the hard solutions to organizational aggravations."

– Kerry Plemmons, Professor of Practice, Daniels School of Business, University of Denver

"Any new idea – by definition will not be accepted at first. It takes repeated attempts, endless demonstrations, monotonous rehearsals before innovation can be accepted and internalized by an organization. This requires courageous patience."

– WARREN BENNIS
American scholar and author of *On Becoming a Leader*

Contents

Forward

When we started to think about rewriting our book, *Brain Disruption: Radical Innovation in Business through Improv*, we knew we wanted to update it with our own business case studies and new academic research – a lot has happened since the first publishing!

Our book *is* a disruption to the brain and its habits. It *is* a blueprint for radical transformation of how organizations do business. It *is* calling out the fundamental methodologies of improv as a foundation to all of this. As we dug into the rewrite, however, we found that the essence of what we do, what we teach, is a new way of **thinking**. Because of this revelation, and the addition of significantly more content, we knew we needed a new title.

Since our approach offers a **mindset change** for the way businesses approach teams, leaders, innovation and culture, it made sense to title the 2.0 version of our book:

The Improv Mindset

In it you will find new examples of client experiences, research and data supporting the powerful impact of this approach, and insightful new content about creating your dream team and the value of increasing your Emotional Intelligence.

Enjoy!

Bruce T. Montgomery
Gail Montgomery

Introduction

"Life is inherently risky. There is only one big risk you should avoid at all costs, and that is the risk of doing nothing."

– Denis Waitley

New ideas. Better teams. Stronger culture. These are the needs you hear from today's business leaders, right?

"Solve this problem."

"Be creative."

"We need a different way to do things!"

It all sounds SO easy.

It *isn't* easy, is it? Thinking *differently* requires a whole new mindset. It means changing our ways to approaching both old and new problems – and then getting the people around us to support and embrace that mindset.

Difficult, right?

We don't think it needs to be. At our company, ExperienceYes, we believe that The Improv Mindset provides the foundation for agility, collaboration, mind-blowing innovation, and dynamic corporate culture.

Let's ask this question: Why do some companies succeed in adverse market conditions while others flounder? For every Pixar or IBM, there are seemingly endless Payless Shoes and Radio-Shacks. What's the difference? What's the secret that enables companies to release compelling new products and services, have a leg up on the competition, develop high-performing teams and create exceptional leaders?

Over the last 20 years, we have developed a keen interest in how some companies can embrace innovation without fear of failure. We've consulted in a variety of industries: healthcare, manufacturing, software development, non-profit theatre, oil and gas, banking, insurance, education, and training and development. Every single one of these industries is looking for answers to the same questions: How can we get our teams to perform better? How can we keep happy employees with a healthy corporate culture? How can we make products that people want? How can we improve our bottom line? How can we *innovate*?

That's where The Improv Mindset comes in. It is the process of altering or shutting down the influence of the brain's "Executive Judge" – that part of the brain that tries to avoid risk at all costs. This area of the brain is an enemy to new ideas, new ways of thinking, and new ways of doing things – **because doing something new requires risk.**

The Improv Mindset is a different approach that combines:

- Divergent Thinking
- Creativity
- Team Performance

- Corporate Culture

There **is** one item that is missing from this list that we feel is the most important item of them all. It's the thing that we've discovered great companies do better than everyone else. They stay agile, flexible and responsive to a constantly changing environment. They use **IMPROVISATION** or "improv."

What is improv? Improv is the act of spontaneous creation. You can make something out of nothing or solve a problem without everything you expect to have. It's a process for saying "yes" to new things without the baggage of fearing the end game. It also happens to be the foundation for comedy groups like *Whose Line Is It Anyway? The Groundlings, Second City,* and *Saturday Night Live.* (Don't worry – we're not going to make you a stand-up comic with this book!)

Through our research and experience, we've found that improv is a powerful business tool that dynamically alters behaviors and the brain. Through it, you can create and establish an **innovative corporate culture** where anyone in a company is both encouraged *and* capable of developing new ideas.

We are uniquely qualified to lead this conversation. We both spent the better part of a decade as professional actors in New York City, where we learned first-hand the importance of divergent thinking and improv. Later, as we developed in our corporate careers, we continued to nurture our passion for improv, ultimately starting our own troupe as well as performing professionally.

The structure of improv rests on four very basic rules:

1) Yes, and...

2) Listen with Intent to Serve

3) Support your Teammates AT ALL COSTS

4) Trust your Instincts

Our experience with improv shined a light on what we felt was a serious skills gap in corporate America. Whether we were leading an IT organization, implementing a large-scale software application, or trying to get a board of directors to finally move in a new direction, there seemed to be no surefire method for getting people to be comfortable in ambiguity. And, not only comfortable, *creative*.

It was hit or miss. People **wanted** to solve problems, they just didn't know **how to be creative or imagine a different path**. They were too worried about failure and the risks that always seemed to outweigh the benefits.

And then it hit us: **improv as a practice** was the perfect method for addressing that skills gap. These rules of improv could work as a business process for employees and companies, and therefore drive high performing teams and foster a culture of innovation and collaboration.

We started asking questions. Why are improv artists able to be so inventive? How do they listen so well and respond so easily to change? Does the continued "practice" of improv increase the ability to be **MORE** creative? We didn't have the answers at the time. We just knew there was something about improv that unlocked intense creativity, agility and performance.

We were inspired. We began researching improv and how it related to the brain. We discovered that there are techniques for disrupting thoughts in a way that increases creativity while suppressing that ever-present Executive Judge of the brain.

We're certain you're familiar with the Executive Judge – it's that nagging internal voice that tells you what you are doing is stupid or ridiculous. It's the part of the brain that's afraid of change and risk, the part that is most likely to run away from new ideas, kill innovation, and destroy team performance.

Through our research of academic studies, we found that improvisers have a way of *dampening the effect of the Executive Judge*. They can enter a mental state where new ideas and creative responses happen "in the moment." Fascinating stuff.

Eventually, we asked this:

1) If we knew this state of creativity that occurs while improvising could basically shut down the part of the brain that prevents new ideas...

...and...

2) Businesses were struggling to find ways to create high performing teams and organizations...

...then...

Could these two things combine to influence a whole new way of thinking?

Several years ago, we launched our consulting company, ExperienceYes, and have since worked with a range of companies from non-profits to the Fortune 500. With them, we've been able to focus on training individuals and teams on The Improv Mindset. It allows for dynamic innovation, builds high-performing teams, solves complex business challenges, and creates healthy cultures. This book is the result of that experience.

As we mentioned earlier, changing your mindset can be difficult. And believe it or not, a large part of that difficulty is caused by that 3-pound gelatinous mass between our ears: our brain. We **want** to have new ideas and imagine alternatives to our "business as usual" concepts. We **know** we need be agile to survive the natural ebb and flow of customer needs and new products. We also know ***change can be painful*** and is often met with conflict and pushback – a struggle that occurs in our teams and organizations, and in our own BRAINS.

Many of these feelings come from our own previous experiences. We've probably all received invitations to corporate brainstorming sessions that began with an email containing hints of desperation about next quarter's projections. Or, perhaps there were those required workshops that focused on fun and interesting ways to help you connect to one another with offerings like "Teamwork 101," "Strength Building," and "The Art of Listening." Chances are that those sessions did little to influence you in the long term.

The Improv Mindset is different. It's not an *"event."* It requires discipline, focus, and practice to free the limitations set by how we think – how our brain stores data, interprets experiences, and habituates our behavior.

Ask yourself these questions:

- How can you trust your co-workers if you don't practice the delicate art of TRUSTING?

- How can anyone feel confident and safe from being judged when everyone in the room has a brain wired for avoiding RISK?

- How can a team be high performers when they've never worked together before, never had clear and concise direction from a leader, and never been celebrated for FAILURE?

You don't solve these things in a 4- or 8-hour workshop.

At a very base level, improv is making something out of nothing. Improv is risk. Improv is change. However, you can't just start improvising and expect that you can hotwire your brain into getting onboard. It won't happen without a change in the way you **think**. In fact, your brain will be running the other direction, trying to find a warm, fuzzy, risk-free place to hide until that crazy idea moves on. It's just safer that way.

What can we do about that? How can we teach ourselves and our companies **to change our mindsets**? We need to alter our thinking and at the same time change how our teams relate to one another. We also need to establish clear rules about how to operate and collaborate.

Consider this book like the recipe for a meal - the ingredients are not new, yet the combination of them is.

This book will help you:

- Learn the rules of improv

- Improve your creativity

- Alter your team's rules of engagement

- Change how you deal with failure

- Increase trust throughout your organization

- Develop a process for having fun

And finally:

- ***Develop an Improv Mindset***

The book is organized into five sections. In the *first section* we explore your brain and how it both facilitates and prevents you from being creative. We discuss cutting-edge research that illustrates how people who are **more creative** are more likely to come up with **good ideas**. By the end of the section, we hope we have convinced you that although your brain is exceptional at mitigating risk, you need to *learn and* *practice* skills that will enable you to think creatively and innovatively.

In the **second section** we focus on the characteristics of great teams. Rarely are we tasked with solving a problem alone. Most of the time we get into a team and make it happen (regardless of whether we're introverts or extroverts). What makes one team more adept at solving problems than another? How can we get our teams to execute tasks better and faster? We discuss The Improv Mindset in more detail and assert that improvisational collaboration is a foundational skill for any great team.

In the **third section** we take a deep dive into the **rules of improv** and how those rules can be taught, practiced, and applied in a business context. We describe the stages through which every team moves, from Forming (the very beginning stage) to *Performing* (the final stage). Improv *accelerates* teams through these stages.

In the **fourth section** we delve into organizational culture. An organization's culture has a direct impact on whether individuals and teams can spread their wings to try new things. The Improv Mindset culture centers on a single word: **failure.** Though it sounds counterintuitive, cultures that encourage and foster failure in an organized and consistent way find more success. This requires great leaders who have tremendous courage in creating a space for people to try something new and fail. Great leaders *want* their people to take risks – even if failure is an outcome. We also discuss methods for integrating innovation into your business processes and the importance of **fun and laughter** (and how improv can improve and influence these).

The *fifth section* lays out the components of ***The Improv Mindset 4i Methodology*** for generating and supporting innovation. The process requires that everyone practices improv, understands the components of listening, and can create something out of nothing.

Throughout the book there are numerous exercises and tools designed to help you and your teams facilitate new and creative thinking. To make these tools and exercises easy to find, they are marked with:

(E) = Exercise

(T) = Tool

———————————————

Keep this in mind: learning and developing The Improv Mindset takes time. Everyone needs to discover, understand and play from the same rulebook before you'll truly see any major change. Companies like Apple, Google, and Pixar allow employees to dedicate some of their work hours to thinking differently. This is not a "read a book and everything will work" approach. You've got to practice, and to practice correctly you need a coach. We are that coach.

Buckle up. It's about to get interesting.

Section 1
Your Brain

"Rabbit's clever," said Pooh thoughtfully.
"Yes," said Piglet, "Rabbit's clever."
"And he has Brain."
"Yes," said Piglet, "Rabbit has Brain."
There was a long silence.
"I suppose," said Pooh, "that that's why he never under-
stands anything."

— A.A. Milne, Winnie-the-Pooh

Before you read any further, do the following exercise. Pull out your cellphone timer or look at the clock and give yourself two minutes. Two minutes exactly. Ready? Now, flip to the next page (Figure 1) and over the next two minutes think of as many different ways that you can use a paperclip as possible. Go.

Different Ways to use a Paperclip	
1)	11)
2)	12)
3)	13)
4)	14)
5)	15)
6)	16)
7)	17)
8)	18)
9)	19)
10)	20)

Figure 1: Paperclip Test

Divergent Thinking

Ever take a test like this before? It's called an alternate uses test (AUT), and it's a common tool for measuring your ability for divergent thinking.

What is *divergent thinking* you ask? How is it different from creativity?

We like Sir Ken Robinson's definition.

"Creativity is the process of having original ideas that have value. Divergent thinking isn't a synonym. It's an essential capacity for creativity. It's the ability to see lots of possible answers to a question. Lots of possibilities to interpreting a question."[1]

With that in mind, how many ideas did you come up with? 5? 10? 30? Most people come up with around 10-15.

What if we told you that there was a study of a group of 1,600 people, and that 98% of that group scored at the genius level? What group of people do you think that would be?

The answer: **Kindergartners**

Why would Kindergartners be SO MUCH better at this test than you? The answer is quite simple: *they don't have the same boundaries that most of us do.*

Look at your list. Did you put down something like "to clip paper together?" Almost every one of our clients gives this answer. But why can't the paperclip be the staff used in The Raiders of the Lost Ark? Or a baseball bat that can knock the earth off its axis? Or a fighting stick for the world's smallest ninja?

If you change the size and material of the paperclip, and give your brain permission to let go of past restrictions you've placed on the object, there's a good chance that you could come up with many more ideas than just 10 or 15.

We don't do that, do we? We are limited by our experience. We know the paperclip to be a paperclip, and our knowledge of the object itself drastically limits our thinking. Kindergartners' brains, on the other hand, are WIDE open and can see no limitations.

---

[1] (Robinson, 2010)

The adult brain is exceptional at categorization. Life could be challenging if we didn't categorize objects and instead, had to relearn what an object did each time we saw it. And once categorized, it's as if our brain says, "A paperclip holds paper together, and it will do so until the end of time."

Clearly there is efficiency to this type of approach. The National Institutes of Health recently mapped the entire brain using functional magnetic resonance imaging (fMRI). They discovered that the brain is actually organized like a grid – a vast superhighway of millions of interconnected neurons containing seemingly endless bits of data. The brain's connections cross at right angles, like the weave in fabric.[2]

We assert that this categorization likely allows us to travel down that superhighway of right angles to access data more quickly. It's like a major city – You want to find meaning of the word "paperclip?" Your brain "pulls out the map," looks for "Objects," turns left at "Office Supplies," then takes a right at "Paper Holders," and finally reaches paperclips! Voila! The location for the definition of "paperclip!"

What happens when we need the paperclip to be something else? What happens when we want to re-categorize, or reimagine, that small piece of metal that holds paper together?

Let's talk about the Kindergartner study again. The researchers performed the study with the same group of 1,600 kids at different times in their development, starting in Kindergarten and following them to adulthood. As the Kindergartners progressed, the data presented some interesting results (Figure 2).

---

[2] (National Institute of Health, 2012)

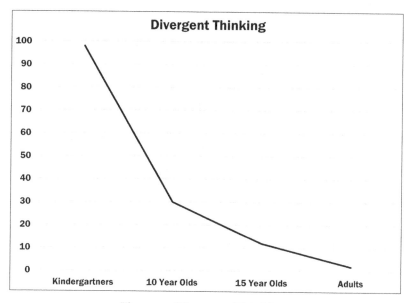

Figure 2: Divergent Thinking[3]

You'll notice that divergent thinking has a very strong trend downward. Think about it – 98% of people tested could come up with genius-level numbers of ideas for a paperclip when they were in Kindergarten. At age 20, only 2% were geniuses. Two percent.

If, at a very basic level, innovation = new ideas, then this drastic drop in idea generation is deeply problematic. So, the question becomes: ***What can we do to disrupt the rigid and natural order of our thinking so that we can come up with radical new ideas?***

---

[3] (Land & Jarman, 1992)

More Ideas = More Creativity

As we defined earlier, **creativity is the process of having original ideas that have value.** Those ideas could be brand new to the world, or tweaks to things that already exist. The important thing is that we need to have a lot of them. The volume of ideas (your ability to keep coming up with ways to use a paperclip, for example) matter. Why?

In a study at MIT, the number of ideas generated was directly correlated with creativity. In the first part of the study, 84 participants (students, professionals, and improvisational comedians) were asked to identify innovative product ideas for a common item, such as a toaster. The participants had only 12 minutes to come up with as many ideas as they could. Ideas included things like optically recognizing burned toast, and a cardboard box solar-powered toaster. The researchers then enlisted a separate group of people to rate the product ideas on five metrics: Creative, Novel, Useful, Product Worthy, and Clear.

In the second part of the study, the same participants were asked to create as many punchlines as they could over 5 minutes to a caption-less New Yorker cartoon (Figure 3).

Figure 3: Sample New Yorker Cartoon

Responses included:

- The company is underwater...and we called you.

- We're expecting the stock market to go to the toilet and may need you for assistance.

- Who you calling beekeeper?

A similar group was asked to rate the legitimacy and humor of the responses.

Researchers then analyzed the results of both tests. What they found was fascinating – the respondents who had ***more ideas also had more creative ideas.*** The researchers concluded that the ability to generate ideas quickly (the more ideas you had within the given time period) was strongly correlated to the creativity of those ideas (r^2 = .82).[4]

Or, put in another way, **the people who had more ideas, had more ideas of value.**

Problems are solved by coming up with ideas. Sometimes a solution is simple and elegant, other times it is overwhelmingly complicated, but it does the same thing: it solves a problem. So, it stands to reason that if we have a method for coming up with lots of ideas, then we are more likely to have an idea that will be good and useful – an idea that will actually "stick." Linus Pauling, the multiple Nobel prize-winning chemist, famously said, "The way to have a good idea is to have a lot of ideas."

Sounds simple, doesn't it? The challenge is that we get in the way of those ideas as we go from being Kindergartners to adults. We are so good at seeing things the way they ARE that we can't see them any other way. It's partly our makeup (how our brains are put together) and partly the way we learn. So, the goal needs to be finding a way to shift the path of our brain's connections so we can increase our flow of creativity.

We can look at this as a process (Figure 4). If you practice improving your divergent thinking skills, we've found that you can increase your number of ideas. Increasing the number of ideas can then increase your chances of finding something of value.

---

[4] (Kudrowitz, 2010)

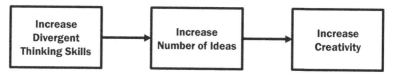

Figure 4: Divergent Thinking Process

Where does The Improv Mindset sit in all of this?

To us, The Improv Mindset is *practical creativity*. It's the process of finding those ideas that have value, and then **applying them to your business**. We will return to innovation later in this book. For now, let's focus on creativity.

Why Does Creativity Matter?

Now, you might at this point find yourself saying, "Great, I need to be more creative. But I can promise you there is nothing creative about what I do at work."

We hear this from our clients quite a bit. Along with, "Shouldn't we just be making money and letting the Marketing team be creative?"

Forrester Consulting, a research-based consulting company, performed a quantitative study exploring how creativity influences business performance. We have always had a suspicion that creative companies outperform their peers (look at Disney, Apple, IDEO), but no real data to back it up. Now we do. The study, entitled *The Creative Dividend*, surveyed senior management from numerous companies that crossed both industries and geographies. The results of the study were astonishing:

- Companies that foster creativity achieve exceptional growth over their peers

- Creative companies enjoy greater market share and competitive leadership (by a factor of 3 to 1!)

- Creative companies win more "great places to work" awards (leading to higher retention rates and employee satisfaction)

The "creative dividend" is real. There are massive dollars at stake here when we're talking about a market share of 3 to 1, and yet 61% of companies do not see themselves as creative.[5] This leaves a HUGE gap (or opportunity) for a company to begin building a framework that is focused both on creativity and innovation, which in turn has the potential to drastically change its position in the marketplace.

And it's not just business where creativity matters. Let's look at professional sports. Researchers in Sweden performed a two-year study on some of their highest-level (national team) soccer players to determine whether there were any factors that could predict the success of the player (as measured by number of goals and assists).

And guess what?

The soccer players who were more creative were more successful in scoring goals and assists.[6]

When you are more creative, your output is better – on the soccer pitch or in the boardroom.

---

[5] (Forrester Research, 2014)

[6] (Vestberg, Gustason, & Petrovic, 2012)

Increasing Your Creativity
and Divergent Thinking Skills

The good news is that there are lots of methods for increasing your divergent thinking skills. Be warned, though, it takes practice.

It's funny – In our workshops we find that our participants freely admit that to learn how to play a sport they need to practice. Think of how long it takes to become proficient at sports like hockey, basketball, or soccer.

"Hours on the field," they'll tell us, "You need to spend hours on the field." Yet, when it comes to creativity, or more importantly our brain, many think they do it just fine. They've got it down. "I know how to get this stuff done, thank you very much." Or, others believe that creativity can't be taught. Some people are creative. Other people aren't. It's that simple.

It IS possible to become more creative, regardless of whether you think you've got it down or it can't be taught. It's done with **practice.** Admitting you need to practice is the first step. You must train your brain to think differently, and the brain will respond.

There is a great deal of current research about neuroplasticity, or the ability of the brain to change and grow (regardless of age).

> *"Every brain is a work in progress. From the day we're born to the day we die, it continuously revises and remodels, improving or slowly declining, as a function of how we use it."*[7]

---

[7] (Merzenich, 2013)

Your brain is malleable! It's a rich, dense and fertile ground that can be exercised and molded.

Researchers at the University of Western Ontario, Canada, found creativity as an actual distinct trainable mental state. Using advanced EEG imaging, they looked at the brains of musicians while they played memorized and improvised music. Some of the musicians had formal improvisation training, and some didn't.

The researchers found several fascinating results:

1) Creativity can be nurtured through immersive training.

2) People who engaged in the practice of an improv-based creative mental state delivered higher quality creative products.

3) **There is significant economic value to developing a creative mental state because the creative results are, simply put, better**[8].

Improv as THE Creative Mental State

We sprinkle the word "improvisation" throughout the book. We like using improv, and more importantly The Improv Mindset, as THE method for increasing your creativity skills and fundamentally increasing your economic value. And it's not just us who are thinking this way.

Researchers at the Universite de Montreal and Florida State University conducted an experiment that analyzed the effects of comedic improvisation ("improv") on elite figure skaters — we're talking the cream of the crop of the figure skating world,

---

[8] (Lopata, Nowicki, & Joanisse, 2017)

the ones who spend hours on the ice and in dance classes while their parents stand off to the side and watch.

In a competition where scores are measured in decimals, it's no surprise that these elite athletes are up for trying almost anything to gain a competitive edge. Think of the work that's been done around other psychological interventions for athletes, such as the power of self-talk, thought control, and mental imagery.

Until recently, however, no one has thought to apply improv to the training regimen for professional athletes let alone business employees.

Think about it: figure skaters take huge physical and artistic risks every day. Who else would be willing to do a triple-toe loop while dressed as a cat in spandex? Suffice it to say, there's inherent risk in ice skating. On the other hand, excessive technique can lead to a somewhat "automaton-like" performance.

So, what interventions allow you to practice failure, take risks, get "out of your head," and laugh all at the same time? Enter improv.

The program took 9 athletes and worked with them over the course of a single season. During the season, the athletes worked with teachers from Cirque du Soleil, who taught them a series of improvisation and mindfulness interventions (10 sessions at 2 hours each).

It may come as a shock that the artistic scores increased for 77% of the participants - and some of those increases were significant! As an intervention, improv is steeped in creativity and self-expression, with an emphasis on taking risks. When you take a risk and it fails, the byproduct is often laughter, and as one of the teachers stated, "developing the athletes' capacity to laugh at themselves was an important goal."

Below are the artistic scores calculated over the season (Figure 5). Check out Participant 9 (P9) who jumped from 3.0 to 4.5. Again, in a competition where decimals matter, this is a HUGE improvement. "It should be noted that the magnitude of the effects was substantial and indicate a positive change in artistic performance and creative attitude and value."

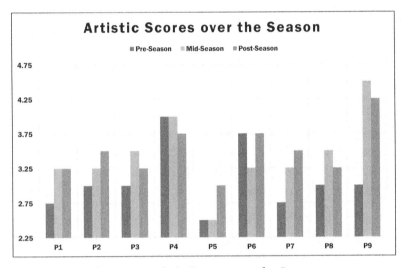

Figure 5: Artistic Scores over the Season

"By learning how to perform freely (using improv), the skaters developed a state that better facilitated and enhanced their performance." You may have heard of this as "flow" or the "flow state."

The researchers also analyzed the overall performance scores over the course of three competitions (Figure 6).

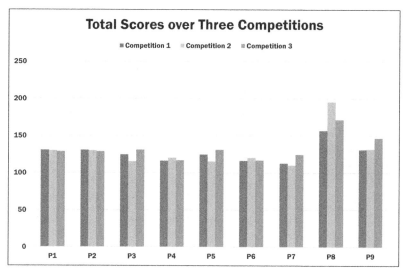

Figure 6: Total Scores over Three Competitions

Though increases appear small, 7 out of 9 of the participants saw an increase - some up to almost 12% in their overall score. This is a phenomenal result with people who are already EXCEPTIONAL at what they do.

With improv, researchers and coaches found that "creativity is an important skill to possess to keep an edge on the opponent."[9]

Increasing Creativity Scores with Improv

Even elementary schools are hopping onto the improv bandwagon. Researchers at University of Surrey in the UK set out to determine whether there are any benefits to "improv interventions" with kids from 10-11 years of age. You'll remember from

---

[9] (Richard, Halliwell, & Tenenbaum, 2017)

earlier in this chapter that kids this age are already brilliant at divergent thinking and creativity.

The researchers divided a group of 34 kids into two groups – an improv group and a non-improv group. All of kids were asked to do a drawing task (an Incomplete Figure Test) that required them to create a figure from a squiggle on a piece of paper. The test was used to assess their nonverbal divergent thinking ability (Figure 7).

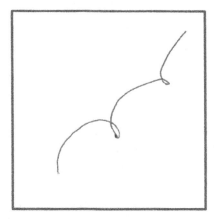

Figure 7: Blank Incomplete Figure Test (example)

Next, the two groups separated and engaged in a series of games. It's important to note that the "improv group" did a series of improvisation-based games, whereas the "non-improv group" did things like "duck-duck-goose."

At the end of the games, all the children took another Incomplete Figure Test (Figure 8).

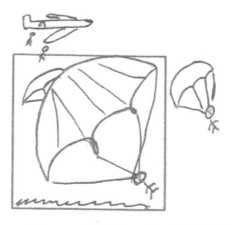

Figure 8: Incomplete Figure Test (filled in)

What was discovered? Well, "improvisation...showed significantly higher post-games originality and elaboration scores."[10]

This means that simply by engaging in improv, you immediately increase creativity.

Your Brain Training Program

As a means of getting you engaged with "training" your brain to develop The Improv Mindset, we've included a 4-week creativity program in the Appendix called *One Month Improv Mindset Training* to get you started. It's a small commitment – maybe 5-10 minutes a day. It's necessary if you want to start the important process of altering and improving your creative abilities. Like hockey or soccer, time dedicated to practicing basic skills will result in improvement over time.

---

[10] (Sowden, Clements, Redlich, & Lewis, 2015)

Section 2
The Dream Team

"The strength of the team is each individual member.
The strength of each member is the team."
— Phil Jackson

Section 1 focused on you, the individual. How are *you* being creative? What is your brain *doing* when it's being creative? However, business does not happen in the vacuum of our brain. It happens at the office. With people. And those people are put in teams with us. And we're supposed to solve problems <u>with</u> them.

So, how do you take this concept of improv and creativity and apply it to a **group of people?** How do you get a **team** to work more effectively in a creative context?

We Built this Team by Picking Straws

Have you ever put together a team before? We mean *really* put it together, where you were thoughtful and could handpick each person for their strengths and input – like you were the head coach of the US Olympic Basketball team. If you were able to put a team together, did it have the perfect distribution of talent, diversity of thought, shared language and understanding of "the rules?"

In our experience, the process for putting together a team in the corporate world is far from Olympian. Instead, it looks like this:

1) Who has the time?

2) OK, no one has the time. So, who's breathing?

Alright, admittedly, maybe it's not that bad. Or, at least, it's not *always* that bad. Teams, and their associated "collaborative work," have become the new norm for businesses today. Oh, sure, you can give teams other buzzword names – committee, task force, solution squad, application geniuses – it's still the same thing: a group of people coming together to collaborate and get things done.

What makes a perfect team? Take a moment and fill in the following table (Figure 9).

Characteristics of the Perfect Team
1)
2)
3)
4)
5)
6)
7)
8)
9)
10)

Figure 9: Characteristics of a Perfect Team

Many of our clients list the following:

- Trust
- Respect
- Common goal(s)
- Collaborate well
- Effective communication
- No judgment
- Diversity of thought and experience
- Everyone contributes
- Have fun

So, here's our question: **When was the last time you really focused on any of the items from this list?** We mean something beyond bowling, drinks at the local bar, or the annual Christmas party – rather, something that worked to fundamentally change the dynamics of how the team behaves, relates to one another, and develops trust.

You might be muttering to yourself, "Please don't tell me that you're going to recommend a trust fall or ropes course."

We're not. Though those are both interesting ways to create bonds between team members. And, what happens four weeks later after those experiences? Traditionally, the team returns to their normal behavior and what was once a great shared experience fades away in response to the daily grind.

What else have you done to strengthen your team?

Most likely nothing. Instead, there's an expectation that teams will simply form, work, and improve, with no real guidance or insight. What does this give us?

Inconsistency. **Great inconsistency.**

Why is that? Inherently, you KNOW what makes a good team – or at least there are countless articles and books that can guide you. And, you also know when you are IN one.

How do you **teach and practice** that?

Team Performance

We made the argument in Section 1 that creativity is important – the more you increase your creativity, the more ideas you have, the **more solutions of value you discover**. And we just discussed the characteristics of the perfect team. What if there was a way to create an environment where some of those characteristics were naturally generated by rules that improve team performance while at the same time increasing creativity skills? Wouldn't you want to *know* that? And, wouldn't you want to **learn** how to use it?

We believe there is one activity that disrupts the brain and makes you better at being creative and better at performing as a team: **improv**.

We mentioned in the Introduction that improv is the act of spontaneous creation. With it, you can make something out of nothing, or solve problems without everything you think you need.

Now, before you drop this book and say, "And that's where you lost me. I'm not doing that touchy-feely stuff," let's explore the rules of improv and the **neuroscience** behind it.

What do you think of when you hear the word improv? Our clients usually say something like:

- Fast-paced
- Funny
- Quick
- No boundaries
- Crazy
- Terrifying (and don't make me do it)

We think of the television show *Whose Line Is It Anyway?* which first aired on the BBC in the late 1980's and later came to the US in the late 1990's continuing well into the 2000's. The format was simple: one host, four performers. In both versions, the host would provide specific situations (with random suggestions collected from the audience) for one or all the performers. The performers would then "improv" their way through a situation.

For many people throughout the US this was their first introduction to improv comedy (though some may be aware of improv troupes like *The Groundlings* in LA and *Second City* in Chicago). The cast of *Whose Line Is It Anyway?* was quite incredible – truly gifted improvisers with a tremendous amount of talent. If you haven't seen them, go google a few of their "best of" collections.

Why were they so good? How were they able to take random suggestions from the audience and turn them into something that was exhilarating and hilarious to watch? How could they think so quickly?

The answer: they followed a structure that has clearly defined rules. Rules that, if consistently applied in a business context, would dramatically reshape how your business performs today.

What are they? (Figure 10)

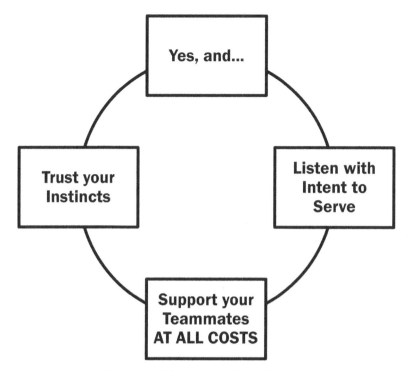

Figure 10: The Four Rules of Improv

Seen anything like these before? You might notice a similarity to the rules of "brainstorming," the technique first created through Creative Problem Solving and the work of Alex Osborn in the 1950's and 60's. Osborn introduced rules for brainstorming – like "defer judgement" and "welcome unusual ideas." You might immediately notice parallels to "Yes, and..." and "Support your teammates at all costs." However, with improv, you practice the rules *outside of the brainstorming session*, as opposed to waiting to when you're in a large conference room and expected to come up with new ideas. In this sense, improv is the **ongoing foundation** for The Improv Mindset, not just the brainstorming event itself.

The researchers from the study out of MIT we referenced earlier found that:

> "...improvisational comedians on average produced 20% more product ideas and 25% more creative product ideas than professional product designers. Furthermore, the few individuals that were highly prolific in both creative product ideation and humorous cartoon caption production had an improvisational comedy background. Many of the games used in improvisational comedy training are intended to promote associative thinking. We designed an improvisational comedy workshop composed of these association-based games. A group of 11 subjects who participated in this workshop **increased their idea output on average by 37%** in a subsequent product brainstorming session. Our findings suggest that improvisational comedy games are a useful warm up for idea generation, that prolific generation is not a domain specific ability and that it **is possible to teach creativity.** Ultimately, this work can lead to the development of tools and methods that designers can use to improve their idea generation skills.[11]

We'll get into greater detail of the rules of improv and how they work soon. Let's talk first about the how and why of improv's ability to open neural pathways within that three pounds of mush between your ears. (No offense. We're sure it's *beautiful* mush.)

---

[11] (Kudrowitz, 2010)

The Neuroscience behind
Improv and Creativity

We again return to your brain before we go any further. Your brain is divided up into many different regions that neuroscientists, thanks to fMRI technology, have begun to map and understand.

There is one phenomenal little part of your brain that loves to control things. It controls things to a fault, in many cases. Although you may not be familiar with its name, we're certain you're familiar with its behavior. It's called the dorsolateral prefrontal cortex (Figure 11), or DL-PFC, and it is responsible for some amazing things related to the executive functions of the brain like:

- Long-range planning
- Risk avoidance
- Working memory
- Inhibition
- Morality

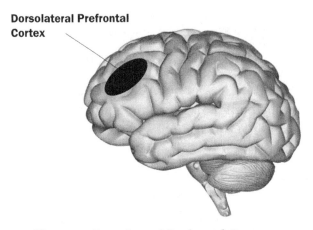

Dorsolateral Prefrontal Cortex

Figure 11: Dorsolateral Prefrontal Cortex[12]

The DL-PFC, or as we like to call it, the "Judge," developed pretty late in the evolutionary game and can be found in both humans and primates. Interestingly, it doesn't finish developing until we're adults – in the early 20's for women and mid 20's for men. (If you've ever wondered why a teenager might be impulsive without fully thinking it through, it's because the part of their brain that readily identifies good vs. bad decisions *isn't even in place yet.*)

So, why is this important to us?

The Judge is great...except when you want to think of new ideas or be creative. It's the part of your brain that tells you "You're acting like an idiot," or "Why would you ever try something like that?" or "Whatever you think you're doing, it's too **risky**!"

Now, don't get us wrong. We NEED that little finger pointing, eye-rolling, restrictive part of the brain to safely function

---

[12] (Brain Clinics, 2016).

in society and to keep us alive. It's just that the Judge is NOT a friend to innovation, risk, and new ideas.

To put it another way: the Judge stifles creativity like a dog muzzle.

Maybe you've had the same experience we've had where you sit around a conference table and throw out ideas. No matter what the idea is, people around the table say things like, "No. We can't do that." "That's impossible." "We've tried that before."

The Judge's natural response is to say "No" first and *maybe* ask questions later. It desperately wants to: 1) Avoid risk. 2) Avoid risk. 3) Oh, and avoid risk.

This is where folks like the cast of *Whose Line Is It Anyway?* have a significant leg up. When they improvise, their brains light up in the areas of creativity and **dampen** the Judge.

They are experiencing ***The Improv Mindset.***

Brain Disruption

Three specific studies have analyzed the brains of improvisers. The first study came out of Johns Hopkins and the work of Dr. Charles Limb. In that study, Limb took accomplished jazz musicians and imaged their brains during four tests. Two of the tests focused on memorized pieces of music (the C-major scale and a piece written for the study). The remaining two tests allowed the musician to riff (improvise) – first on the C-major scale, and then against a recorded piece of music.

The results showed that, when allowed the freedom to create their own music,

"...the brain turned off areas linked to self-monitoring and inhibition and turned on those that let self-expression flow. In addition, the brain regions involved with all of the senses lit up during that time of improvisation, indicating a heightened state of awareness — performers literally taste, smell, and feel the air around them. Most fascinating about this aspect of the scans was their uncanny similarity to patterns seen during deep REM sleep, creating a tantalizing notion of a connection between improvisation and dreaming."[13]

So, a jazz musician who is improvising can quiet his/her Judge and allow the creative parts of their brain to activate. They actually suppress the Judge!

The second study came out of the National Institute on Deafness and Other Communication Disorders (NIDCD) in Los Angeles and focused on freestyle rap artists. Freestyle rapping is often performed as a battle on a stage in front of hundreds of people. A disc jockey (DJ) plays a beat-driven musical track, and each rap artist creates various rhymes off the beat. The requirement: the rhymes must make sense and are most likely in response to whatever the other rapper has said. Through this process, the rappers weave in complex stories about their impressions of each other, their rap styles, and (occasionally) their mothers. The point is that it's all improvised right on the spot. (You can google "rap artist battle rounds" for examples).

Like the Johns Hopkins study, the rappers were analyzed under an fMRI. First, they were given a beat and asked to perform a memorized, well-rehearsed series of lyrics. Second, they were given the exact same beat and asked to freestyle.

---

[13] (Westbrook, 2016)

The researchers saw a similar pattern in the brain of the rappers as compared to the jazz musicians. Take a look at the chart below. You'll note that when the rappers freestyle, just like the jazz musicians, they dial down the Judge and dial up the parts of the brain that are involved with creativity (Figure 12).[14]

---

[14] (Liu, et al., 2012)

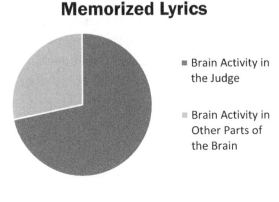

Memorized Lyrics

- Brain Activity in the Judge
- Brain Activity in Other Parts of the Brain

Freestyled Lyrics

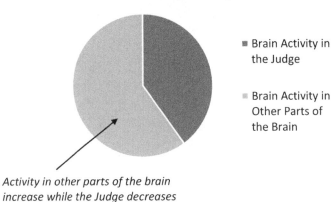

- Brain Activity in the Judge
- Brain Activity in Other Parts of the Brain

Activity in other parts of the brain increase while the Judge decreases

Figure 12: Comparing the Brain during Freestyled and Memorized Lyrics

How do they do this? Well, they temporarily "turn off" that part of the brain that's constantly judging and constantly telling them "this is stupid" in order to create something new.

The third study was also run by Charles Limb, and this time out of the University of California, San Francisco where he is the Chief of the Division of Otology, Neurotology and Skull

Base Surgery. We know a lot about this study because HE ASKED US TO PARTICIPATE IN IT. Yep, the picture below (Figure 13 & Figure 14) is Bruce followed by Bruce's brain (no HIPAA violation here).

Figure 13: Bruce in front of a fancy MRI machine

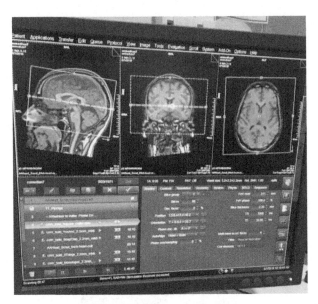

Figure 14: Bruce's Brain

We can, with certainty, confirm he has a brain. (Note: as a part of the study they also imaged Colin Mochrie's brain from *Whose Line Is It Anyway?* fame. We can confirm that he has a brain, too.)

Like the other studies, the research process focused on imaging the brains of comedic improvisers while doing memorized and improvised tasks. Rather than a new song or new lyrics coming out, crazy voices and even crazier situations were captured.

And, similar results were recorded![15] All three studies found a positive correlation between a change in activity in the Judge and the ability to create things out of mid-air. The people

---

[15] (Barret & Limb, 2020)

who could suppress the Judge were better at activating the creative parts of their brain.

How can *you* do this? Again, let's call back to the MIT study on improv from earlier in this section:

> *"We found that a group of 11 students individually generated on average 37% more ideas after an improvisational workshop."*[16]

You might be saying to yourself, "Great, but I'm no Miles Davis. I can barely think of what I should buy at the grocery store."

Well, what if you had a way of ***practicing*** changing the dynamics of your brain? Regularly disrupting the Judge so that it gets out of the way, making those new ideas more readily available?

That's where improv, like the kind practiced by the cast of *Whose Line Is It Anyway?* comes in.

Improvisational Collaboration

Think of the last time you truly worked *collaboratively*. We mean the kind where you were having a conversation that sparked an idea...and someone else built on that idea ...and then someone else built on that idea...and so on. No one was judging. No one was over-thinking things. You were just working together.

High performing teams play off one another. They listen and react. They DO things instead of waiting until things have been planned out to the "nth" degree. No "analysis paralysis" there.

---

[16] (Kudrowitz, 2010)

What types of teams come to mind when you think of *collaboration*?

We think of the Japanese cooking show Iron Chef. The Iron Chef started in the early 1990's and ended in 1999. It pitted a master chef (known as an Iron Chef) in a specific cuisine against a challenger.

 At the beginning of the show the challenger would pick which Iron Chef they wanted to battle. Then, the secret ingredient of the day would be revealed. The ingredient would serve as the basis for four to six dishes the chefs (and their assistants) made over the course of the next hour. We personally loved the ingredients – they included things like squid, conger eel, and Chinese cabbage – foods that are far afield from our Western eating experiences.

After the chefs finished cooking, three celebrity guests, including film stars and food critics, would rate the dishes and a winner would be crowned.

To be honest, the winner never mattered to us. What mattered most was what the chefs *did* in the kitchen during their cooking time. Remember: these chefs had only one hour to create four to six dishes with an ingredient that was only JUST revealed to them. The dishes had to taste great, look beautiful on the plate, and have a well-balanced flavor profile.

Each Iron Chef had a small group of 2-3 assistants. The Iron Chef would quickly identify what the team would make, then set them off to work. Like a well-choreographed dance, they would cut, chop, sear, bake – and constantly collaborate.

Every member of the team knew where they were going and what the others were working on. And, if something went wrong, they adjusted and changed course immediately **together**. Soufflé just fell? Quick, turn it into a sauce. Have a bunch of black ink you just took from the squid? Use it as an ingredient in the ice cream (yes, this actually happened). Overcooked the asparagus? Throw it in the blender with some peppers and make an asparagus salsa.

The important thing is that they never stopped. They were constantly *improvising as a team* – changing and creating, creating and changing. And when they failed, they pivoted to something else without letting failure stop them. No one said, "I can't believe you just did that." It was more like, "OK, we just lost that dish. Now, what do we do?"

Can you think of other good examples of teams that improvise in a similar manner? How about any fast-action sports team, like basketball or hockey? Each sport requires a team that has practiced and worked together over time, and it's usually obvious which teams have practiced more when they get out on the ice or court. Out there, the team might be trying to execute a structured play and must respond and react to changing conditions all the time. We would argue that a vast majority of plays that are practiced outside of game time are never fully executed, which means that great teams respond as if they are living and breathing as one and IMPROVISE.

What about sports teams and their ability to improvise **creatively?** We don't often even bring those words together: team sports and creativity. Teams that are improvising creatively TOGETHER are higher performing teams. Period.

Let's look at a specific sport: soccer (or football, if you live anywhere else in the world than the US). You've likely seen the game – two teams of 11 work to kick a ball through a goal (and they can't use their hands). From a creativity standpoint, it doesn't seem like all that much can happen – you kick the ball, someone else stops it, controls and kicks it. Rinse and repeat until you score a goal.

Researchers in Germany found something compelling with regards to creativity in soccer. They analyzed all the goals of the 2010 and 2014 FIFA World Cup and the UEFA Euro 2016. Basically, they had several experts sit down and watch the last 8 actions that occurred on the field before a goal was scored.

Using ratings mechanisms for measuring creativity, the experts evaluated the plays and determined that "teams that advanced to the later part of the tournament demonstrated greater creativity."

In other words, the teams that were more creative WON, and "creativity seems to be a factor for success in high-level soccer."[17]

Why does this matter? *With improvisational collaboration, you must practice being creative together so that you're ready when it counts.*

In another study at Stanford University's School of Business,

> "...they found that the most innovative teams were the ones that spent less time in the planning stage and more time executing – instead of planning, they improvised. Contrary to what many managers believe, the more

---

[17] (Kempe & Memmert, 2018)

time a group spent planning in advance, the slower pro-ject development was."[18]

Why do you think that is? Well, the more you talk and plan and THINK about things, the more opportunity your brain must activate that Judge. The more the Judge gets its hooks into the process, the more likely it is that new ideas get shut down.[19]

In order to suppress this regular engagement of the Judge, you must practice improvisational collaboration.

Let's extend this concept further (beyond the team) to legitimate business performance. Researchers at the Universiti Utara Malaysia looked at the role of improvisation within the manufacturing sector of over 200 small- to medium-sized businesses. The hypothesis was simple: The stronger the role of improvisation, the better the corporate performance. And that's precisely what they found.

Companies that know how to improvise outperform their peers.

The result of this study means that "decision makers...need to consider implementing improvisational practice in their organizations in order to gain and sustain superior firm performance."

---

[18] (Sawyer, 2007)

[19] (Arashad, Zakaria, Kadzrina, & Ahmad, 2018)

Want to Change your Teams? Increase your Emotional Intelligence with Improv

We are often called in to work with teams when they are getting ready for their pitch or big presentations. We support them in imagining situations to help them prepare for the unanticipated. There's always a need for quick thinking and dealing with surprises (like what to do if a fire alarm goes off before you start, or if the most important buyer gets up and leaves after 10 minutes, or if your electric toothbrush goes off in your bag while you're giving your pitch...we could go on).

In our opinion, business success includes good emotional intelligence, which is built on the foundation of good improv.

What is Emotional Intelligence, or EI?

EI is "the capacity to be aware of, control, and express one's emotions, and to handle interpersonal relationships judiciously and empathetically."[20]

Peter Salovey and John D. Mayer came up with the term "Emotional Intelligence" in 1990 and described it as *a form of social intelligence that involves the ability to monitor one's own and others' feelings and emotions, to discriminate among them, and to use this information to guide one's thinking and action.*[21]

They also began a research program to *measure* EI and to determine its importance. In one study, they found that when individuals who were more in tune with identifying and nam-

---

[20] (Leadum, 2018)

[21] (Bechtoldt, 2017)

ing moods, watched a film with upsetting content, they recovered faster. In another study, people who ranked higher in their ability to perceive, comprehend, and identify others' feelings were much more capable of responding to shifts in their environments and created strong social bonds and networks.

Inspired by Salovey and Mayer's work, Daniel Goleman published the book *Emotional Intelligence* in 1995. As a science writer for the New York Times, Goleman specialized in brain and behavior research. He was interested in the concept around how cognitive and intelligence tests did NOT predict business success. Rather, there were certain characteristics of *emotionally intelligent* people that did, which are (Figure 15):

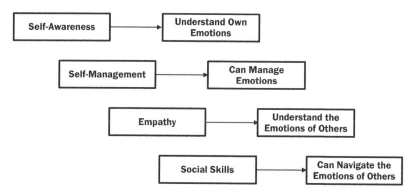

Figure 15: Components of Emotional Intelligence[22]

We find that more and more companies are looking to increase EI for their leaders and teams. This is not surprising, given the unique by-products that a high level of EI can create, including:

---

[22] (Golis, 2013)

- Greater influence with clients in sales, customer success, marketing, and internally across functional teams
- More effective leadership and management
- Powerful elicitation and listening techniques
- Quicker decision making and stress management
- Ability to resolve problems and manage conflict
- Higher salaries

Inside organizations, business teams with high EI resolve conflict faster, break down barriers between functional teams, and develop trust and respect for one another. Managers can be more effective in executing strategy. As a result, many businesses are even integrating EI testing into their hiring practices.

A leader needs the strength and competence to inspire, motivate, and drive their teams toward success. Without the benefit of high EI, they struggle to pave the way for successful collaboration. A leader's ability to notice and understand their own emotions, and the emotions of others, helps enable the team drive to a shared goal. To truly manage *people*, you must *understand* them.

More importantly, EI can have an impact on the bottom line. Organizations that have employees with high EI report that customers have an increase in feeling heard, valued and connected on a personal level. They feel less like they are being "sold" to, and more like they have partners in "solving" business challenges and needs. Finally, there is recognition that intentional development in the associated area of EI for individuals, teams and leaders is a ***key differentiator***.

T *What is your Emotional Intelligence?*

Let's take a moment and give you a chance to check your EI. Fill out the answers to the questions in the table below (Figure 16).

Question	Rank (1 = Low, 5 = High)
1) I have a good understanding of my own emotions.	1 2 3 4 5
2) I can control my temper so that I can handle difficulties rationally.	1 2 3 4 5
3) People tell me that I'm a good listener.	1 2 3 4 5
4) I can always calm down quickly when I am upset or anxious.	1 2 3 4 5
5) I enjoy organizing groups.	1 2 3 4 5
6) I am quite capable of controlling my own emotions.	1 2 3 4 5
7) I know both my strengths and my weaknesses.	1 2 3 4 5
8) I don't mind conflict or negotiating.	1 2 3 4 5
9) I ask people for feedback on what I can improve.	1 2 3 4 5
10) I am a good observer of the emotions of others.	1 2 3 4 5

Question	Rank (1 = Low, 5 = High)
11) I build rapport with others quickly.	1 2 3 4 5
12) I use active listening skills during conversations.	1 2 3 4 5

Figure 16: Adapted from How Emotionally Intelligent Are You? Questionnaire[23]

Now take the results and plug them in the following table (Figure 17).

Description	Steps	Value
Total Score	Total of the values for questions 1-12.	
Self-Awareness	Total the values from questions 1, 7, 9.	
Self-Regulation	Total the values from questions 2, 4, 6.	
Empathy	Total the values from questions 3, 10, 12.	
Social Skills	Total the values from questions 5, 8, 11.	

Figure 17: How Emotionally Intelligent Are You? Results

---

[23] (Law, Wong,, & Song, 2004)

What is your total?

- 12-25: We recommend that you focus on your EI. You may find that you are overwhelmed in stressful situations with your emotions getting the better of you. Or, you may not be comfortable with conflict. After you're upset, it may be difficult to calm down.

- 26-45: On average, you could use some improvement with your EI. You likely have good relationships with only some of your colleagues – others can be more challenging. The focus should be on working on *your relationships*.

- 46-60: Your EI is right where it should be. That shouldn't stop you from continuing to focus on improving!

It is important to note, that this is a self-assessment and we often "fool" ourselves into believing things we *want* to be true. Many EI websites have opportunities for you to invite others in assessing you. You should consider that for a more comprehensive score.

With your score in mind, here are some recommendations for improving in the four EI areas.

Self-Awareness: Start to recognize internal emotions and feelings you have in response to others in one-on-one conversations, meetings, or informal gatherings. When you get irritated or angry by something, ask yourself "Why?" and begin to tease out the reasons for it. If you find yourself laughing at someone and others aren't laughing, it may be because it isn't an appropriate response. If you find yourself angry after someone takes credit for something you did, dig in and reflect.

Self-Management: This can be one of the more difficult elements of EI to regulate because Self-Management deals with instinctual responses. Because of this, changing the way that we *react* by regulating our *response* can be hard. Being aware is the first step.

Additionally, consider simply giving yourself some ***time*** before you respond. Allowing for some quick reflection to evaluate your gut response can help to avoid negative situations. And if you recall the "rules" of improv in the previous section, "Listening with the Intent to Serve" becomes a natural way to support this goal. Don't worry, we'll look at this in more detail in Section 3.

Empathy: This is clearly a fundamental skill for good EI and requires that you recognize both the emotions and perspectives of other people. To develop your empathy abilities, start focusing on other's viewpoints. Imagine how they might feel. You've likely heard the term, "walk in their shoes."

When you ask questions, use silence in the space after a question to allow others to provide the answer and express their emotions. Avoid interrupting them (see the Five Second Rule exercise in Section 3).

Social Skills: People with good social skills are exceptional at being truly present and understanding what the emotional dynamics are in a room. It requires that you open yourself up *externally*. Challenge yourself (and your teams) to start focusing on things in a more concentrated way. For example, when someone is talking, or telling a story, begin to take either mental or physical notes of the things you see and hear. Some questions you can ask yourself are:

1) What are they doing **physically** with their body that tells me about their mood or emotional connection to the words?

2) What am I **hearing** in the tone of their voice that gives me clues to how they feel about the topic? Are they quiet? Loud? High-pitched?

3) What *facial expressions* am I seeing that would indicate their mood, emotion or connection to the story?

4) What **emotions** can I see, hear, and sense from the other person speaking? What clues are there?

Learning to micro-focus on these facets of conversation, storytelling and verbal interactions is a key skill in social awareness. And, for an extension of this, you can ask yourself these same questions when you are working on your *self*-awareness. Then, work on managing your outward physicality, tone, and expressions.

When it comes to social skills, all the hard work you have done in the three previous facets of EI will develop your ability to elicit more information and detail that helps you influence others. Using the Four Rules of Improv will naturally lead you to enhancing your social skills in helping others to be heard, acknowledged, validated and respected.

Here's a great example of excellent social awareness and social skills: One of our clients (we will call her "Wendy") likes to tell a story of when she and her team had a sales pitch go south. This was a multi-million-dollar opportunity, and the pitch was being held at a swanky office in New York City. She flew in five experts after weeks preparing for the presentation.

They arrived early and ensured everything was set up and ready to go. And then they waited. Finally, after 15 minutes past the start time, the potential client showed up clearly frazzled. Wendy is on the sharper end of the EI scale, and she could tell the client was unusually distracted and not ready to be pitched. So, she did a very simple thing: she commented on it. "Hey, it looks like there might be some things you need to focus on that are outside of this meeting. Would you like to reschedule?"

Two things happened here:

1) Wendy acknowledged what everyone else was feeling in the room.

2) She was willing to invest in having everyone come back in order to allow for better timing of the presentation.

And you know what happened? The client THANKED HER and said "Yes, that would be better."

Turns out that the client was having a family crisis and was trying to manage around her day before she could get to the hospital where her daughter was recovering from a bicycle accident.

Ultimately, they held the meeting two weeks later and secured a $10M contract. Wendy read the room, identified there was a problem, and brought it up. Classic Emotional Intelligence at work.

We see a direct correlation between EI and improv. Mindfulness and "in the moment" attention is required for both. The rules of improv organically increase EI. How? Let's dig into this:

- Yes, and... supports the acknowledgement and validation of others and brings trust and common ground for collaboration, understanding and connection.

- Listening with Intent to Serve continues to strengthen the trust between individuals and is an impactful way to gather information both intellectually and emotionally to better inform. It also affords time for self-awareness and self-management processing.

- Support your Teammates AT ALL COSTS provides opportunities to build strong relationships with teammates, continues to strengthen trust between teams, and builds your social awareness.

- Trust your Instincts is your gateway into self-awareness. Being in touch with *your* gut reaction and feelings toward something can bring deeper insight to your personal motivation.

Greater EI benefits individuals, teams, leaders and companies. It's a win-win.

Researchers for the Journal of Relationship Marketing found that **Emotional Intelligence** and the **ability to improv** directly influenced sales success and outcomes.

They looked at the importance of this within the *team* selling environment. Specifically analyzing whether teams that knew how to improvise more effectively won more contracts.

Most commonly, improv occurs during Q&A sessions. This makes sense as buyers have a chance to ask questions and hear how the seller responds. And buyers often attempt to ask questions that can deliberately "trip up" the sales team. Q&A also allows buyers to see the team dynamic in action – who answers questions, are they collaborative and cohesive, etc.

"Improvisation helps buyers gauge how effective the selling team will be in handling the unexpected during the actual project they are being interviewed for."

Look at some additional specific buyer quotes regarding improv (Figure 18):

Figure 18: Sales Team Quotes

Buyers are LOOKING for how you and your team improv together.

Through interviews and associated surveys, the researchers collected data from a broad base of buyers and sellers, as well as several groups of engineering consultants and related teams (Figure 19).

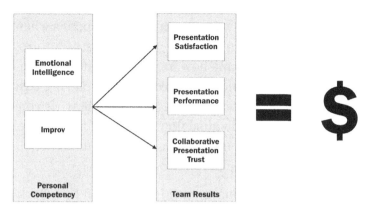

Figure 19: EI and Improv Conceptual Model

"Given these important findings, it would be beneficial for managers to attempt to foster improvisation in their existing sales force and in their selling team recruiting process. Managers should consider sales training that emphasizes improv. Managers should also foster programs that assess a team member's EI abilities and set up appropriate EI training and development programs."[24]

More Flow = More Joy

In the 1970's, Mikail Csikzentmihalyi began exploring the concept of a "flow state." This is the what happens in your brain when you have a strong singular focus on something, and all sense of time and awareness just slips away. It might happen for you when you're meditating, or perhaps gardening, or when macramé-ing an afghan blanket (hey, we grew up in the 70's. The struggle was real).

---

[24] (Hill, Bush, Vorhies, & King, 2017)

We often think of flow as something that happens when we are by ourselves, and in the mid-90's and early 2000's researchers began to examine flow in a social context. Much has been written about the flow that occurs while playing basketball, performing jazz, or dancing. This "social flow" is considerably different from individual flow because of the complexity and dynamics of human interaction. And, our fundamental response to social flow results is more joy.

Researchers at St. Bonaventure University in New York examined singular versus group-based flow. They ran several experiments that started with a series of surveys and ended with groups playing pickleball alone and together (pickleball is a smaller version of tennis played on the interior of a tennis court).

Not surprisingly, researchers found participants reported more flow and experienced more joy when they were working together in groups. They had an "emotional contagion that is expressed by people who must work face-to-face interdependently and cooperatively."[25]

This is one of the things we love about improv. Within a very tight group framework, it provides the space and the intervention for that emotional contagion. Improv is all about social flow. You need to listen and be in the moment, and you need do it *together*.

Improv is often about solving a problem that's in front of you. Sometimes, that problem is something like "I need to justify being a kumquat farmer standing on the edge of a cliff in the Swiss Alps." And the social nature of the improv team is that *they are going to help you do just that.*

---

[25] (Walker, 2010)

The end result is that you experience great joy when you do it. Lots of joy. Trust us.

Your Teams Should be Child-like (Not Childish)

Remember back in Kindergarten when the teacher would ask a question and every single hand would shoot up to answer it? 34 hands and the occasional "Ooh, ooh, pick me, pick me" coming from the entire group was a common sight for teachers.

When we were young, failure had no cost. We didn't associate it with anything negative and no one cared if we were wrong. The possibilities in life were endless and vast, and we were fearless. Limitless in our capacity for invention and in our potential to shine.

Now fast forward a little and remember back when you were a high schooler. When the teacher asked a question, how many hands shot up? One, maybe? Two? As we grew older, there were increasing consequences and social pressures related to our leaps of faith, and fewer and fewer hands were raised. We lost our sense of play and started labeling and compartmentalizing everything into categories. Fear had fertile ground in which to dominate our thoughts and we became limited by our own beliefs and understanding of the world.

Guess what? Researchers are starting to analyze the fact that the ability to PLAY, even as an adult, is critical for creative success and The Improv Mindset.

So, what *is* play when it comes to adults? Researchers have defined play as "a state of mind reflected in behavior in every tiny action. When you are immersed in this mood, you are open to experience pleasure, discovery, knowledge, and creativity."[26]

You know "play" – it usually involves a completely immersive experience where you're working on something creative, you're in the moment, and you're having fun. Maybe it's happened for you when you're playing a boardgame with your family, or when you're jumping into a foam pit that you KNOW is for toddlers and you just couldn't resist, when you've started a food fight, or poked fun during a karaoke party.

This is what makes improv so powerful – it naturally brings the process for playing together **_with_** solving problems. And, "by necessity the participants need to work collectively to develop solutions that in some cases may stretch participants outside their comfort zones, thus providing opportunities for growth."[27]

E *Draw and Pass*

Here's a fun exercise that you can do with a group to get them into the mind of being in a "state of play." Ideally you should do this exercise with 6-10 people. This is based on the popular game "Telestrations," which is essentially like a visual-based telephone game.

Hand out a stack of stapled together blank sheets of paper to each participant (the number of sheets of paper should equal the number of participants). Ensure that each person has a pen.

---

[26] (Hassan, 2019)

[27] (O'Neill, 2016)

Start by having each participant think of words to write down on the first blank sheet of paper – for example, the name of a movie, a tourist attraction, a food, a phrase etc.

Next, have the participants each write down their item on the first sheet of paper, and ensure that no one can see what they've written. For example, let's say that I write down "Lady and the Tramp."

Everyone flips over their booklets face down and passes them clockwise.

Once the booklets have been redistributed, each person flips over their new booklet and reads what has been written. (Remember, mine was Lady and the Tramp." Let's say you're on my left and I pass it to you.)

Then, each person flips over to the next sheet of blank paper in the booklet and begins to draw what they've just read. They have one minute to visually reflect on the item and create a picture. It's important to note that they CAN'T USE WORDS on the picture. Back to our example – because I gave you Lady and the Tramp, you might draw the famous spaghetti scene where they kiss for the first time (Figure 20).

Figure 20: Lady and the Tramp Example

Once the minute is over, each participant turns the booklet facedown and again passes the booklet clockwise.

So, in our example, you just passed your picture of Lady and the Tramp to the person on your left and you've also received another booklet with a completely different picture on it.

Everyone looks at their new booklet and tries to determine exactly what the item that was drawn is. Then, they flip over to the next blank sheet of paper and write down their guess. In our case, here's what the person on my left wrote down (Figure 21):

Figure 21: Lady and the Tramp –> Spaghetti

They pass the booklet clockwise again and each person tries to draw what was "guessed" in the previous step. This continues until your first booklet (the one you started with) makes it all the way back to you.

You then reveal each page to the group, starting with yours and going to the end.

Ultimately, you'll find that the original item has changed drastically by the time you finish. After the Lady and the Tramp went through the entire group, the transitions looked like this (Figure 22):

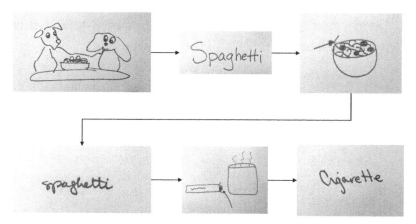

Figure 22: Lady and the Tramp – Completed

There are a few of great things that come out of this exercise:

1) The drawing component combined with the lateral thinking that occurs when you are trying to figure out the picture of what you were handed, engages a completely different part of the brain.

2) It limits the experience of feeling threatened in a group setting – even if someone can't draw at all.

3) People laugh. A lot.

E ***Skill of Clarity***

Another exercise for getting groups into a state of play is to focus on the skill of clarity. Think again back to your Kindergarten days. If the teacher was not exceptionally clear with instructions to do simple tasks, mayhem followed. We're the same way as adults.

Divide your group into smaller groups of 4-5. For this exercise you'll need a table with the following items:

- A new jar of peanut butter

- A new jar of jelly

- A paper plate

- A knife

- Two slices of bread

- A note card and pen for each group (for writing instructions)

Give each group 5 minutes to log the instructions on the note card for making the perfect peanut butter and jelly sandwich.

As facilitator, collect and review the responses from each group and pull one set of directions that may have a step or two missing, or a complicated set of descriptions.

Ask one of the groups that did not write the set of instructions you chose to come forward to the table. Select a volunteer to read the instructions.

The group now making the peanut butter and jelly sandwich must follow the instructions VERBATIM. For example, if there is a protective cover on the inside of the jar of peanut butter, the instructions might not have suggested that the protective cover must first be removed. Therefore, the team must continue trying to perform actions to get peanut butter on the knife with the cover still in the way.

The point is that even with simplest of tasks, we can neglect very obvious steps, or leave steps open to interpretation. By using play and fun to solidify the skills necessary for high-performing teams, leaders, and individuals, it offers opportunities for all to connect meaningfully.

Section 3
The Four Rules of Improv

"In the long history of humankind (and animal kind, too) those who learned to collaborate and improvise most effectively have prevailed."

– Charles Darwin

I t's hard to believe we would need *rules* in improv – it seems like an oxymoron. Things are just supposed to happen, right? There **is** structure to improv, and we need rules. Think about it like this: to yield the most consistent results and to get to the good stuff of trusting and free-form creativity, we need a framework – something that we can hang our hats on that all of us can understand. Rules give our teams a shared and common language.

And, as we've been saying, we need to *practice* those rules by doing exercises, just like a hockey player or an Iron Chef.

In this section we are going to explore how specific rules are applied in the kind of improv practiced by *Whose Line Is It Anyway?* and *Second City*. We will look at each rule in detail and then discuss how these rules can be applied to the world of business.

The Four Rules of Improv are (Figure 23):

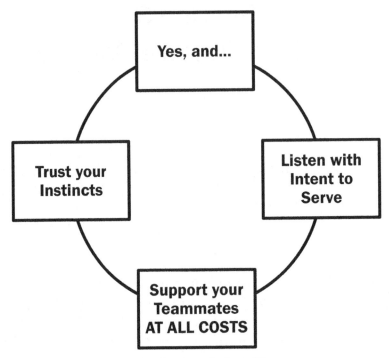

Figure 23: The Four Rules of Improv

They look really simple, don't they? They ARE simple. They just take some effort to perfect.

Rule 1: Yes, and...

Yes, and...

How many times a day would you say that you utter the word "No?" 10 times? 20 times? 100? (If you're a parent, the number most likely increases exponentially!) Contrast that number with how many times you say the word "Yes." If you're the average person, you'll find that the difference might be 10 to 1, or even 20 to 1. (We aren't talking about how we say "YES" to too many things and can't manage our time effectively. This is a different topic we will cover later – it IS possible to say "Yes" to people and still manage your time.)

We are exceptionally good at saying "No," both in life and business. The word "No" helps us protect our own skin. We practice saying it every day, over and over, in part because the Judge is constantly guiding us away from risk.

Let's look at a business example where NO played an important role: Blockbuster video. Remember the days of standing in line to rent a video? The days when Blockbuster would guarantee that they had the latest title out and charged absolutely outrageous late fees? (We're fairly sure we put a kid or two through college with those late fees.)

In 2000, Netflix CEO Reed Hasting hired a private plane, flew out to Blockbuster and pitched selling a 49% stake in Netflix in order to become Blockbuster's digital streaming service. They'd even take the name Blockbuster.com. At the time, Netflix only had 300,000 subscribers, and the bursting of the dot.com bubble was still fresh. Blockbuster famously said,

"No."[28] Today, Blockbuster is nearly out of business and Netflix is...well, a multi-billion dollar company and the first choice of many for streaming a movie or series online.

You might be saying to yourself, "Yeah, but that's just business. Blockbuster made a business decision with the information they had at the time. Good or bad."

And you might be right. It's easy to be an armchair quarterback and say, "Well, they should have done X or Y." However, maybe, just maybe, if their executive team practiced the process of "Yes, and..." their brains may have been more prepared for thinking creatively, and they would have seen the opportunity in a far different light. It happens. We've seen it.

Let's explore the other end of the spectrum. Let's look at a company that has "Yes, and..." tied to its corporate DNA: Pixar, Inc.

> *"The process of bringing the skills, ideas, and personality styles of an entire team together to achieve a shared vision...is critical to the process of generating ideas and solving problems"* at Pixar. **'Yes, and...' is part of Pixar's common lexicon that fosters creativity and keeps the vibe and energy in the room upbeat and alive.**"[29]

And it's no wonder (at least to us) that improv is integrated into the core curriculum at their Pixar University!

Looking at their box office receipts, you can see why this might be important. ***Pixar is tremendously profitable***.

---

[28] (Auletta, 2014)

[29] (Capodagli & Jackson, 2010)

Their typical cost for making a movie averages $96M, yet their Box Office receipts worldwide average $655M. ***$655M!***[30]

Not bad for a little animation company, right?

We believe that everyone could use a little of that Pixar magic in their businesses, and one way to spark that magic is by focusing on the same thing Pixar does: "Yes, and...."

So, how does this "Yes, and..." thing work?

As we mentioned earlier, you're already great at saying "No." "Yes," on the other hand, takes work and discipline because it often requires you to take a risk and try something new or something that you aren't even sure how to do (something that Blockbuster was unwilling to do).

The main concept of "Yes, and..." in improv works like this: You have to say "Yes" to anything that's given to you. It's that simple. If someone is working through an exercise and says, "Check out this pineapple," you can't say, "No, that's not a pine-apple. That's a baby." Or, if someone says, "Whew, it's so cold right now," you can't say, "No, it's hot." Instead, you must acknowledge what the person just said with a "Yes," and then ADD to it with the "and...," which means you are adding to whatever was originally given.

For example, in response to "Check out this pineapple," you might say, "___Yes___, it's beautiful. ___And___ I'll bet you win the competition today." With this, you've accepted the pineapple AND added to the creation – a competition. Now your partner has a whole host of options to "Yes, and..." the competition aspect of the scene. Maybe they're worried about losing. Maybe they've

---

[30] (the-numbers.com, 2020)

grown the absolutely perfect pineapple. Maybe they're plotting their revenge against mean Mrs. Bates.

The response to "Whew, it's so cold right now," might be, "**_Yes_** it is. **_And_** I can't believe you brought us to Antarctica, Captain Shackleton." Again, you've said "Yes" and added to the scene by establishing who the person is and where you are.

The possibilities are endless as long as you say "**_Yes, and...._**" The possibilities stop as soon as you say "No." **_The Improv Mindset is all about possibility._** Saying "No" is all about control, and letting go of that control can be extremely difficult.

There are a couple of exercises that we like to use that can help get people into the habit of saying "Yes, and...."

Yes, Point, Walk

The first exercise is called "*Yes, Point, Walk.*" With this exercise, groups of up to 15 people stand in a circle facing in, shoulder-to-shoulder. One person (we'll call him "Jack") points at another person ("Paige"). When Paige realizes she is being pointed at, she must make eye contact and say "Yes" back to Jack.

Then, two things happen simultaneously. Jack (as soon as Paige has said, "Yes") begins walking to take Paige's location in the circle. Paige must now point at another person in the circle (Tom) and wait for Tom to say "Yes." This is important: Paige cannot move until Tom says "Yes" – even if Jack makes it all the way into Paige's space. This continues for several minutes until everyone in the circle has had a chance to move to different locations.

You can add a layer of difficulty by having everyone do the exercise silently – people only point without saying "Yes." And finally, you can do it without ever pointing, just eyes making contact.

This game ALWAYS stumps our participants. They get the order of things wrong. They say "Yes" when they point instead of when they are being pointed at. They get in a hurry and forget to say "Yes" to the one pointing at them. And the biggest error of them all, they start moving to the "new" spot before they have the acceptance from that person.

Though simple, this exercise can have very powerful results because the group is practicing saying "Yes" to anyone in the circle.

Let's dig a little deeper into those errors. This exercise can be incredibly enlightening when it comes to your team's weaknesses.

The basic act of "accepting" the point from the other person seems to be the first struggle. The participant is often so busy thinking and preparing for the next part of the exercise that they have intellectually and physically moved on to the next step. In our experience, this is an indication of a lack of trust in the other person and/or in themselves, a lack of understanding of the directive, and the inability to stay present. Teams can fall victim to this when there is a goal set for them, and one or more of them rush to get started with the tasks BEFORE they have a comprehensive understanding of all the guidelines or requirements. It's similar to when we were in school and there were those couple of students that rushed through the instructions to get to the test, completely missing that the correct way to title their page or fill out their name ended up counting for a large percentage of their grade.

Another mistake in this activity occurs when someone has accepted the "point," then senses the other person coming toward them and therefore feels compelled to move before they have connected to another team member with their own point and received a "Yes." The pressure of having someone moving toward them, ready to take their spot, is too much and they lose the objective of their next step(s). We liken this to the anxiety team members can feel when they are sometimes forced to "drop" a task in order to get something else done. The burden of knowing there's a deadline associated with their next task causes them to leave the other task incomplete.

With practice, this exercise teaches the basic process for saying "Yes" over and over. Think of it as a warmup for your daily workout.

Look, I have a...

Another exercise for practicing "Yes, and..." is called "Look, I have a..." In this exercise, everyone pairs off and stands face-to-face with their partner. One person (we'll call her Alice) starts by saying, "Look, I have a..." and then follows it with anything that comes to mind. And we mean *anything*.

For example, she might say, "Look, I have a pirate ship." The second person (we'll call him Frank) responds back with "Yes, and...," and builds onto that original thought. For example, the second person might say, "Yes, and I can't wait to board her, Captain. I'll go get the oranges."

Once the response is done, Frank then starts with his own "Look, I have a..." idea that is completely unrelated to the first "Yes, and...." So, Frank might then say, "Look, I have a washing machine that's broken." And Alice might respond with, "Yes, and it's your fault that we never have any clean clothes for the baby." This continues back and forth for several minutes.

The point of the exercise is two-fold. First, you have to say "Yes, and..." no matter how crazy the first idea is. Second, you build on the idea regardless of what is given to you.

Does this exercise apply in a business setting? Yes! Remember: coming up with new and innovative ideas requires you to think and act differently. You must disrupt the natural cycle of the Judge in your brain, which is constantly moving you away from risk. With practice, saying "Yes, and..." moves you toward something new, something different, and something potentially risky.

It's fascinating to see how this concept of "Yes, and..." plays out with our clients. After a few gentle corrections to identify when someone has said "No," the team always seems to begin self-policing. We've had administrative assistants call out CEOs when the "Yes, and..." rule has been violated.

Months later, we've had those same CEOs tell us that "Yes, and..." has been adopted as a standard meeting practice.

"No" and "Yes, but..."

Remember how we mentioned earlier in this section that people are naturally compelled to say "No?" The effects of the word itself can impact team dynamics in significant ways. Think about what happens when you're trying to build a team or perform a task. Having someone standing over you saying "No, that's not right," or "No, we shouldn't do it that way," has a negative effect. What would happen on a hockey team if every time the puck was passed to a specific player, that player refused the puck and knocked it back the other direction. And, yet, persistent use of the word "No" occurs in the corporate world all the time (think of your last business meeting).

Researchers at the Brookhaven National Laboratory analyzed what happens in the brain when we hear a "No." Using fMRI, they found that when you process a "No," the regions in the brain that control anger light up. Additionally, your reaction time takes a nosedive – meaning that whatever you're doing at the time, it then takes you *longer to do* because you must change gears to get your brain back into the task. So, every time you hear a "No," in that moment *you are less engaged, lose momentum and struggle to get back to efficiency.*[31] Understanding that there are real consequences at the neurological and physical level when we hear "No" continue to support the need to say "Yes, and...."

At this point you might be muttering to yourself, "But I just bought a book that teaches me how to say 'No' so that I can decrease my stress levels and increase my free time!" and here we are encouraging you to work on saying, "Yes, and...." Hang in there, we'll address how to use "Yes, and..." to soften a "No" in the next subsection.

If you step back and look at the prevalence of the word "No" within organizations or corporations, you can imagine its negative impact on corporate culture (we discuss culture in more detail in Section 4). At a fundamental level, "No" affects every person within an organization, pulling down anyone that is practicing The Improv Mindset.

---

[31] (Alia-Klein, et al., 2007)

Here are two exercises that can help you and your team to notice the pervasiveness of the word "No."

E *Count the number of times you say Yes/No in a day.*

This exercise works best if you get your entire team to participate. Simply count the number of times you say "Yes" and "No" in a day. Try to be mindful of all your conversations – texts, emails, face-to-face, etc. At the end of every day, document the numbers for the entire team. Try and do this for one week. We suspect that the numbers will surprise you. Later, after you've become more comfortable with The Improv Mindset, perform the exercise again and see if there is any difference in the Yes/No distribution. You will almost certainly see a levelling out of the two words as team members begin to see the negative effects of saying "No," and get much better at saying "Yes."

E *Identify when people say "No" to you*

This is a twist on the previous activity. Flip your awareness and track the number of times you *receive* the word "No." Make note of how many times you hear "No" from co-workers, family, friends, and other people in your everyday world. Can you identify any themes for why "No" was the response? Themes might include: time of day, how you are asking the question, and whether the question was asked with other people present or alone.

By the way, there is another way that we say "No" without being aware that we're saying it. The phrase "Yes, **but**..." essentially does the same thing as "No," it's just a bit more subtle.

- "I believe we can get this prototype to market by next quarter, but we can't sell it until June."

- "That was a great report, but the format is all wrong."

- "Yes, we could do what you're asking, but there's a big presentation coming up and no one has the time."

With "Yes, **and...**" and a simple tweak of the language, you can change these comments to support The Improv Mindset. For example, the last comment in the list above could be "Yes, we could do what you're asking, **_and_** we'd better adjust the time constraints."

As you're working through the last two exercises, consider adding "Yes, but..." to the overall counts of "No." And then make attempts to remove it from your everyday language.

One More Comment on Yes, and...

We often get a lot of skepticism about "Yes, and..." when we start our workshops. We recently worked with the executive team of a large hospital, and you wouldn't believe the amount of eye-rolling and comments like, "Yeah, you don't know our company." This can be a tough concept, in part because the Judge is fighting the concept itself.

Our point is that you need to open yourself up and get better at saying "Yes, and..." to things because you're already fantastic at saying "No." Remember, the possibilities are endless as long as you say, "Yes, and...."

Occasionally, someone will ask, "What if we **HAVE** to say "No" to something?" Well, then, say "No" to it. Making a decision that will jeopardize your business? Yeah, say "No" to that.

Illegal activity? Say "No" to that, too. The point is to **get into a more consistent mindset of saying "Yes, and..." and see what changes**.

We also encourage the practice of saying "Yes, and..." even when you admit you can't do something. In some instances, you may have to say "No" based on the timing of a specific request. For example, Mark has a huge deadline he is trying to meet, and a co-worker asks him to help with another project. Here's how this situation could go down:

Sally: "Mark, could you give me some support on the Thompson proposal?"

Mark: "No, I have a deadline for Wayfair, and I am committed until the end of the week."

Or,

Mark: "I'd love to BUT I am swamped with Wayfair."

What if the conversation went like this?

Sally: "Mark, could you give me some support on the Thompson proposal?"

Mark: "Yes, and I have some free time early next week. Will that work?"

Now, if that doesn't work for Sally, she still feels that Mark was willing to help – not that she's being denied. Yet, in a way, that's just what Mark did. He was honest in saying he could support her with the project and the timing was bad for him. Then, he gave her a realistic timeline for helping her.

Sometimes, you might try using the "Yes, and..." as a means of showing your understanding of what they are asking.

Sally: "Mark, could you give me some support on the Thompson proposal?"

Mark: "I know that this is important to you, Sally. (That's the YES, part.) I think John has some time today to help you get it squared away. (That's the AND part. See what we did there?)

Let's try another example – one of our clients, a multi-billion dollar energy company, was trying to figure out a new way to standardize how to design and build production facilities. Their current model was based on uniquely designed facilities for each specific location. From a functionality standpoint the design was great – each design was perfect for its spot. However, from a scalability standpoint it took forever to execute because everything was custom designed. Vendors couldn't pre-design anything because they wouldn't know what to build. As for maintenance, every site was different, from the equipment down to the nuts and bolts. Challenging, right?

The company brought in a diverse group of people from their organization to think through the problem – field techs, engineers, designers, and regulatory advisors. And they wanted us to help them.

One particular sticking point was around regulatory compliance. With so many legal constraints and permitting requirements surrounding energy companies, going fast seemed nearly impossible. There was no way to get "creative" around regulations and it became very easy to default to "No." What could be done?

By becoming aware of "Yes, and...," and practicing it diligently, the team was able to focus on specific limitations within the regulations themselves. They discovered together that there were ways to influence regulatory decisions and timing, which would help them dramatically increase their speed to market on certain projects. "Yes, and..." kept the possibilities open without getting caught up in "Well, it's a regulation, so there's nothing we can do." Instead, it was: "Yes, that's a concern. And, we could work on lobbying to change that."

Additionally, we guided them through several workshops focused on an analysis of current practices with regards to their designs. Through the use of "Yes, and...," they determined that a few modifications to the prefab engineering process would be less expensive than the customizations they'd been making to each location. They went from an attitude of "We've always done it this way," to asking and answering questions like "What could be changed?" and "Is there another way?" This started a conversation that was so exciting that nearly every person in the room was on their feet with a dry erase marker in hand creating the new design.

Ultimately, they made such radical changes to their design that they estimated that they would *save more than ten million dollars in their first year of implementation.* If you knew that simply changing your language would save you money, would you do it?

Rule 2: Listen with Intent to Serve

> **Listen with Intent to Serve**

A lot has been written about listening and the importance of improving listening skills. Look through a *Harvard Business Review* or any issue of a leadership magazine and you'll probably find an article on listening. Most of what has been written is about active listening, which involves:

- Demonstrating that you're listening (making eye contact, nodding, saying, "uh huh" occasionally)

- Clarifying points with open-ended questions

- Improving the physical environment (distractions, location)

However, this isn't a book on active listening. It's a book that discusses the skills for **actually** listening, which is different from "active" listening, and a rarity in business today. In a recent survey, a group of corporate executives were asked to rate the most important skill for today's workforce, and 80% said it was listening. Many of those same executives said that listening was the area where most improvement was needed for their workforce.[32] We would argue that, despite widespread "active" listening, businesses continue to identify deficits in listening as one of their biggest concerns because people are not **actually** listening.

Listening in improv is a critical skill, and it's practiced in two ways: listening to *serve* your teammates and listening to yourself (which we will explore in Rule 4: Trust your Instincts).

---

[32] (Salopek, 1991)

Candidly, most of us listen with the intent to *respond*. You know the drill – someone is explaining something and all you're doing is waiting for them to take a breath so that you can get a word in. We are poised to *speak* and rarely have the sensitivity or awareness that the real value in communicating is discovering how you can help each other.

Listening is an area that can be especially challenging for our clients. Just about every team we've worked with suffers from a lack of good listening skills. Why is that?

Because listening can be tough.

Let's look at it this way. When you're in a team you have great ideas. You just know that they're great. As soon as someone else is talking, however, you don't have a chance to articulate your ideas. Now it becomes a battle – "Get my ideas out there before the other person does. Because mine is the best." There's an inherent selfishness that counteracts quality listening.

Ever have that experience around a conference table? You're in a room with one, four, or ten other people trying to solve a problem, and everyone is trying to speak. Because, after all, you are brilliant and have brilliant ideas.

Or, maybe you're on the other end of the spectrum. Maybe you feel that you simply *can't* speak because everyone else won't stop talking. Or that it isn't worth forcing your idea into the discussion because you can tell that people aren't really listening to each other.

The skill of listening in improv isn't about getting your ideas out OVER someone else's. It's about acknowledging input and creating something together with your partner or team. If you're in the driver's seat, and only in the driver's seat, you'll never get the perspective of what it's like to be a passenger. And sometimes you'll need to be a passenger.

Here are some interesting facts about listening:

- 85% of what we know we have learned through listening

- Humans generally listen at a 25% comprehension rate

- In a typical business day, we spend 45% of our time listening, 30% of our time talking, 16% reading and 9% writing

- Less than 2% of all professionals have had formal education or learning to understand and improve listening skills and techniques (less than 2%!!!)[33]

There are a few exercises that are particularly good for encouraging listening. One exercise is called "The Five Second Rule."

Five Second Rule

In this exercise, two participants are asked to come to the front of the room. Let's call them John and Jenn. The group provides a suggestion for how to get a two-person scene started. For example, a moderator might ask for an item that is typically stored in a hall closet. The answer could be a ski helmet. Now John and Jenn start a two-person scene with "ski helmet" as their jumping off point.

---

[33] (Goodall, 2015)

The secret to the scene, however, is that neither of them can say anything without waiting for a full five seconds after the other player has spoken. The exercise might play out like this:

John: Man, it's cold. I can't wait until we're on the slopes. I'll at least be able to work up a sweat.

Five seconds go by.

Jenn: I'm already sweating from that walk from the car.

Five seconds.

John: Well, you still look beautiful to me.

Five seconds.

Jenn: Wow. That's quite a compliment for a first date.

Five seconds.

John: Look, I thought skiing would be fun. Active, you know? Your online profile said you were outdoorsy.

Five seconds.

Jenn: I meant that I like to go outdoors. Sometimes. Not actually BE OUTDOORS DOING STUFF!

And so on.

This exercise is productive because it prevents the participants from piling ideas onto each other while at the same time giving space to each idea before moving on.

It also highlights those people who tend to railroad ideas. They, in particular, have a tough time adhering to the five second rule without opening their mouths.

We often use this exercise when we are conducting a brainstorming session. We start by having everyone stand in a circle, facing each other. We announce whatever problem we're working on and ensure that everyone has a clear understanding of it. Then, the group takes turns either coming up with a new solution or responding to a solution that's been given to the circle, following the rule that ***there must be five seconds before each response.*** Also, everyone must participate at some point.

Here's an example from a customer service client of ours:

Moderator:	We need to improve client wait times on the phone without increasing our staffing.
	Five seconds.
Participant 1:	It seems like there are two approaches to me: technology and process. Or some combination of both.
	Five seconds.
Participant 2:	Yes, and process is most likely the cheapest of the two to fix.
	Five seconds.
Participant 3:	OK, so if we focus on process...What keeps our agents from resolving the call within the first two minutes?
	Five seconds.

Participant 1:   Training? Maybe they don't know how to answer?

Five seconds.

Participant 4:   Don't we have a huge database with lots of answers that they can search?

Five seconds.

Participant 5:   How complicated is it to search?

Five seconds.

Participant 2:   I think it's OK, as long as you know what you're looking for.

Five seconds.

Participant 4:   Has anyone in here actually used the tool?

Five seconds.

Participant 6:   I have. It's tough.

The session went back and forth from there, and the team uncovered that the customer service search tool was particularly burdensome. Only a few employees knew how to use the tool effectively. The few who did were also the employees with the best response times. In addition, because the customer service reps were compensated for being in the top five for response times, the top performers were not motivated to teach their co-workers how to use the tool. The top performers could lose out on their bonuses!

By the end of the session, the team had worked out a plan to address training around the tool, identified ways to fix the bonus compensation, and assigned super users to work with IT to improve overall usage.

The Five Second Rule can be a very powerful tool because it requires people to stop jumping in, allows time for participants to hear and process what is being said, and encourages people who typically would not participate to speak up.

From a customer perspective, allowing for more time in between often allows for more information sharing. People don't naturally care for silence and will fill it. This is a fantastic thing when you need to know MORE about your client's needs. Remember, it's about *serving* them.

Also, it can offer support in your Emotional Intelligence development. Adding time to process your thoughts, feelings and perceptions can be the lifeline you need to choose your next words more wisely.

Conducted Story

Another tool we use to develop listening skills (and overcome listening challenges) is called Conducted Story. The exercise begins by identifying a group of four or five participants who come to the front of the room. They face the rest of the group while standing in a tight semi-circle, as if they are a small choir. The moderator is responsible for "conducting" the story. A participant may speak only when the "conductor" points at them and must stop speaking immediately when the conductor stops pointing at them, whether it's mid-thought, mid-sentence, or even mid-syllable.

Once everyone is in place, the exercise begins with the conductor asking the rest of the group for a title to a story that has never been told before. Once identified, the title is then repeated by the four or five people standing at the front of the room. For example:

Conductor:	May I have the title of a story that's never been told before?
Audience:	The Hummingbird and the Moth.
Conductor:	The Hummingbird and the Moth. Thank you. Choir, please repeat.
Entire Choir:	The Hummingbird and the Moth.

The Conductor then points at one of the choir members. That choir member MUST speak and start telling the story of The Hummingbird and the Moth.

Choir 1:	There once was a hummingbird that had a broken wing...

And so on from there. When the Conductor stops pointing, that person stops speaking. When the Conductor points at someone else, that person starts speaking and must continue the story right where the other person left off.

Now, this is one of those exercises that can really go anywhere – it totally depends on what the Choir comes up with. And there is NO WAY anyone can predict where the story might go.

The critical point, however, is that the Choir members **must** be listening to each other for the story to make sense. If they are spending time trying to think of the next thing to say, or designing where the story will go, they will miss their chance to add a logical next part to the story.

This exercise is particularly good at identifying moments when people aren't listening. For example, here's someone who didn't listen to what came before.

> **Choir 1:** There once was a hummingbird that had a broken wing. He was very sad that he'd broken his wing and was sitting on the edge of a...

The Conductor stops pointing, which forces Choir 1 to stop. The Conductor then points to Choir 2.

> **Choir 2:** The moth hated the hummingbird.

You can see that Choir 2 didn't follow along and finish the sentence to "sitting on the edge of a...." Rather, they jumped to a completely different part of the story. If this happens, it's necessary to call out the behavior so that those listening skills can continue to be developed.

The point of both the Conducted Story and the Five Second Rule is this: You must **practice listening to each other** to ensure that you move the story forward. Each exercise can identify when members of a team are listening to one another and when they're not. Listening is something that we all assume we do well, and the truth of the matter is that all of us could probably use help.

Note that listening is closely intertwined with the rule "Yes, and...," because you can't say "Yes" to something if you didn't hear it in the first place!

Rule 3: Support your Teammates
AT ALL COSTS

Support your Teammates AT ALL COSTS

We often feel like there is a life or death component to improv. Yes, we know this is an exaggeration. And, in improv, it's crucial to support your teammates with the commitment that you either fail or succeed **together.** There's no "individual" – you are all working to create something that you couldn't have created alone.

Let's look back at our Iron Chef example. If one member of the Iron Chef team makes a mistake by burning a giant sea scallop, it doesn't help anyone to stop and have a team meeting to analyze the mistake or why it's important not to make mistakes. Instead, team members gather, improvise a solution, change directions, and **MOVE ON.** (Yes, that happened, and...)

Something similar could be said of great basketball teams. If a play goes wrong, the team resets and gets ready for whatever comes next. There's no time to stop and discuss. Later, in practice, they'll work on drills to prevent whatever went wrong the time before. In the heat of the moment, they understand that mistakes are part of the game – maybe today will be your turn to make one, and tomorrow it might be someone else's.

Now, you might be thinking, "Well, come on, businesses are a little different. It's not a game or a reality TV show." Yes, and the importance of *supporting your teammates* should be just like the behavior of a great basketball team. You need to celebrate the good decisions, support the bad decisions, and move on.

Take a moment to think about the teams that you're on right now at work. Is there that kind of commitment and support? Do you, right now, support your teammates AT ALL COSTS? Do they provide that kind of support for you?

We'll bet not. Your corporate culture may encourage something more like, "I'm just trying to not get stabbed in the back," or "Team? What team?"

Do you remember the characteristics of a perfect team that we wrote down in Section 1? They included things like:

- Trust
- Respect
- Common goal(s)
- Collaborate well
- Effective communication
- No judgment
- Diversity of thought and experience
- Everyone contributes
- Have fun

In our opinion, the most important characteristic is the first item on the list: trust. Trust is the core component of "Support your Teammates AT ALL COSTS." In improv, when someone walks out and says there's a giant walrus right in front of you, they need to trust that you won't say, "I don't think so. It looks like a snail to me." They must trust that you'll "Yes, and..." that walrus and move forward, and you must trust that they'll do the same.

Trust is a tricky one, though, because we know at a fundamental level that trust is *earned*. And, **through the practice of improv**, you can run drills and get better, just like a basketball team or the Iron Chef. When you are consistent with your "Yes, and..." and you listen with the intent to SERVE, trust is a natural by-product.

E *One Line at a Time*

This is a quick exercise that is designed for 4-10 people. It requires a whiteboard and some different colored whiteboard pens. The goal of the exercise is to have the team draw a creative image together, one line at a time.

To start the exercise, one person steps forward and draws a single line on the board. It can be straight or curved or squiggly. Then, a second person steps forward and adds another line that adds onto the first line. A third person steps forward and adds a third line. And so on.

The exercise is complete when all team members agree that the image is finished, which most likely takes two or three cycles through the entire team.

As you might have guessed, this exercise is predicated on Rule 1: Yes, and.... Once a line is drawn it can't be erased. It's up to the next person to find a way to support and justify whatever was put up there.

Also, there's almost no way to control the direction of where the drawing is going to go. You accept that whatever was in your mind when you put your line up there will be totally different by the time it gets back to you.

E *Tallest Tower*

A second exercise for practicing Rule 3: Support Your Teammates AT ALL COSTS is called The Tallest Tower. We like to set up this game as a competition between multiple teams of 4-5 people. The goal is simple: the group that builds the tallest tower wins. And we offer the winners something of value – usually individual $10 gift cards to a nearby coffee chain. This helps raise the level of the competition because they are working toward something that they want to win.

We start out by giving each group the same materials. Typically, the materials consist of what is listed below, although you can improvise with whatever you might have available – as long as every team has the same items. Inside of a large Ziploc bag, we include:

- A paperclip
- A straw (in wrapping)
- A binder clip
- Two sticky labels
- Two wooden coffee stirrers
- Chopsticks
- Two index cards
- A pipe cleaner

The teams have 10 minutes to build the tower. The tower must be freestanding (not affixed to the table) and stay upright for 30 seconds once the 10 minutes are over.

And there's one more rule: For the first four minutes the team **discusses** their approach for building the tower **without touching the materials.**

This exercise can illustrate many things for the team. First, the competition aspect adds a layer of immediacy and stress, much like the Iron Chef. People can act differently (good or bad) when they are competing.

Second, there will be team members that are more comfortable in the "discussion" portion (the first four minutes) than the "build" portion (the last six minutes), and vice versa.

Third, the exercise will allow the competitors to use their newly learned rules of improv. The materials will NOT work like they expected or planned. They will have to **support** each other through determining a new solution.

In this activity, there's a great deal of information for them to gather. How will these materials respond once we get our hands on them? Do we know what these materials weigh? What are our roles? Will someone be the "builder" and others give advice? Has everyone given input? And on and on...

Then, once in the thick of building the tower, questions to ask include: Are they listening to one another? Are they supporting each other in saying "Yes, and...?" Are they able to be agile in their thinking of what they should do if what they originally intended isn't working? Are they exhibiting trust?

The Mousetrap of Death

This exercise is useful for building trust and support. It is ideal for a team of 4-5, so divide your group as necessary.

You'll need the following items per team:

- A blindfold
- 9 pennies
- 5 mousetraps
- A package of thumbtacks
- A table

Before meeting with the group, disable all the mousetraps except one. Regardless of how you do it, each of the disabled mousetraps should appear real and set.

Have each team pick a person to be blindfolded. This person can't be told about the mousetraps being disabled. The rest of the team will individually provide instructions to the blindfolded person.

Move the team to standing in front of a table, then ensure that each blindfolded person cannot see. Explain the following:

- The goal of this exercise is to collect the coins off the table
- Each person on the team will take turns giving a single instruction to the blindfolded person
- As you distribute the thumbtacks and pennies on the table, state "I have spread coins and thumbtacks all over the table. As an added level of difficulty, I am also putting down mousetraps"

- As you pull out the mousetraps to place on the table, grab the one mousetrap that has not been disabled and accidentally set it off so that everyone in the room hears the telltale "snap" of the trap. Then state, "This one is obviously too sensitive. The other ones are ready to go"

- Place the tripped mousetrap to the side and distribute the what-looks-like-active mousetraps around the table

- One at a time, each member of the team gives instructions one at a time to the blindfolded person to guide them in picking up all the coins. For example, "Feel for the edge of the table with your right hand." Then, "Now that you are touching the table, keep it on that plane and move your index finger forward two inches." And so on

This exercise will enforce active listening by sharing both the goal of safety for the blindfolded person and gathering the coins successfully.[34]

Rule 4: Trust your Instincts

Trust your Instincts

The last of our four rules, "Trust your Instincts," is all about allowing yourself to trust the first idea that pops into your head. It's the consistent practice of tamping down the Judge and stepping out to take a risk and try something new or different.

---

[34] (VanDerveer & Butterick, 2016)

Strangely, we find this flies in the face of the culture at most companies. Our entire lives we've most likely heard the phrase, "THINK before you SPEAK." And, honestly, that's a really important part of being a healthy functioning adult. It can save our jobs! And, we're not talking about this in a setting where you need to be truly mindful about what comes out of your mouth. We're talking about using this rule when you innovate, brainstorm, and problem solve. Those are the times when you can't afford to think through and question every word like you would for a boardroom presentation. You can't allow that self-editing part of you to get in the way of creativity.

Researchers at a European University found that people have innate instincts when it comes to creativity, and as you get older you grow more likely to mistrust those instincts. Yet, these instincts are exceptional at providing insight into solving problems. The study found that people who dare to investigate different ways of thinking and to be open to alternatives are more likely to actually solve something that's challenging.[35] So, the better you are at trusting those instincts, the better you will be at dealing with that next wall that's in front of you.

 ### First Word, Best Word

One exercise for building the skill of trusting your instincts is called "First Word, Best Word."

In this exercise a group of 5-10 people stands in a circle, facing in. Everyone starts clapping quietly or snapping to an established beat. Once the group is clapping/snapping in unison, one person states a single word in rhythm. The person on their left says a single word that relates to the word that was just said.

---

[35] (Nelissen, 2013)

Then everyone says the words together, followed by "Da-Duh-Da-Duh." The person who stated the last word begins with a new one, and this continues around the circle until everyone has had a chance to do it twice.

It looks like this:

Everyone begins snapping.

Person One (in time with the snapping): Pickle.

Person Two (in time with the snapping): Jar.

Everyone: Pickle-Jar. Da-Duh-Da-Duh.

Person Two: Standing.

Person Three: Tall.

Everyone: Standing-Tall. Da-Duh-Da-Duh.

Person Three: Skinny.

Person Four: Jeans.

Everyone: Skinny-Jeans. Da-Duh-Da-Duh.

Person Four: Pickle.

Person Five: Sky.

Everyone: Pickle Sky. Da-Duh-Da-Duh.

It's critical that participants don't overthink their responses. They just state whatever comes into their brains in the moment. There's NO time to prepare. If they think too much, they'll be off rhythm.

And the words don't necessarily have to make sense. It's completely acceptable as teams are working on this skill to see:

Person Four: Pickle.

Person Five: Sky.

Everyone: Pickle Sky. Da-Duh-Da-Duh.

The point is to **keep it going.**

This exercise is ideal for setting up the foundation of brainstorming sessions. When you brainstorm you want people to have the freedom to say anything in response to something else. You want the ideas to flow. The rhythm and the speed of this exercise force people to listen and respond, without taking time to determine whether it's the "right" response.

We typically add one more layer to this exercise once everyone gets comfortable with it. We alter the rules so that the words CANNOT relate to one another. It might look like this:

Everyone begins snapping.

Person One: Tree.

Person Two: Pants.

Everyone: Tree-Pants. Da-Duh-Da-Duh.

The point is that the participants should be listening closely in order to respond in rhythm.

E Make a Game

Another exercise for trusting our instincts is called "Make a Game." In this exercise the group is divided into teams of 4 to 5 people. They are all given the same materials you might have lying around at home or in your office. We typically use:

- 15 Lego® bricks of varying sizes and styles

- A deck of cards

- A pair of dice

- Chopsticks
- String
- Paperclips
- Post-Its®
- Pens
- Ketchup packets

The teams have 20 minutes to make up a game that they will demonstrate to the rest of the group. They must use at least four of the materials, although they can use more if they want. At the end, the game that is the most fun to play, as voted on by the rest of the groups, wins.

"Trust your instincts" comes into play as the teams begin their creative process. Invariably there are two types of teams: the team that **plans** and the team that **does**. Can you guess which team is typically the winner? The doers. The doers are the first to start throwing out ideas and trying things.

This is an important point: the teams that trust their instincts and get to DOING almost always win.

The Importance of the Rules

As you might have guessed, the rules of improv are closely intertwined. For example, if you're doing almost any of the exercises we listed above, it's impossible to say "Yes, and..." if you're not listening to what's being given. And it's difficult for you to trust your instincts if you're not getting support from the team or saying "Yes, and...."

So, why is the practice of these rules so important? Why do they matter?

In business, we have high expectations of our teams. We want them to get out there and solve problems, innovate, and make our companies more profitable.

We've found that teams that practice these rules shorten the time it takes to complete tasks, trust each other more, and listen better.

In the 1960's, Bruce Tuckman identified four stages of group development that every team goes through as they work toward completing any task. Those stages are: Forming, Storming, Norming, and Performing, and each stage is defined with specific characteristics (Figure 24).

Forming	Storming	Norming	Performing
• Team meets each other for the first time • Orientation • Establish ground rules • Polite • Members are treated as strangers	• Express opinions as individuals • Resist control • Infighting over leadership, definition and norms • Demotivation	• Accept other's viewpoints • New roles are adopted • Personal opinions are expressed	• The group becomes capable • Flexible • Open • Supportive • Trusting • Solutions emerge

Figure 24: Tuckman's Stages of Team Development[36]

In today's fast paced business environment, we are moving into and out of teams quickly. The practice of improv allows team members to accelerate through these various stages of group development by establishing a shared language and framework for developing trust, new ideas, and acceptance.

---

[36] (Tuckman, 1965)

Think about it: Imagine if everyone in your company already knew and practiced the rules of Yes, and..., Listen with Intent to Serve, Support your Teammates AT ALL COSTS, and Trust your Instincts?

By learning and practicing the rules of improv and developing The Improv Mindset, the first three stages of Tuckman's model are compressed, allowing your teams to accelerate through to becoming higher performing teams faster.

Tuckman's model, then, looks like this (Figure 25):

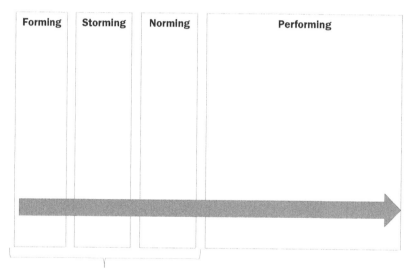

Acceleration

Figure 25: Tuckman's Model with Improv Mindset Acceleration

Remember those improvisational collaborators we discussed earlier? Let's look back at the hockey example. Envision if every time you put a hockey team together, the team members had to learn (or re-learn) the rules of the game. They'd need to learn how to hold a hockey stick, what the "puck" is, and how to score a goal. It would be a nightmare.

Now imagine if the hockey team you're bringing together already understands how to play, can ice skate, and knows what happens during an "icing" penalty. The results of this team would be drastically different than the inexperienced team. We KNOW that.

So, why do we expect success from our business teams without teaching them the rules of the game? Especially when we know that those rules would improve how they perform together?

If you could increase the speed at which you could get teams to the Performing stage by 10%. Or 25%. Or 50% - now *that* would have a giant impact on your business.

You can do that with ***The Improv Mindset***.

Section 4
Culture

"An organization's ability to learn, and translate that learning into action rapidly, is the ultimate competitive advantage."

– Jack Welch

U p to this point we've been discussing the brain and new ideas somewhat myopically by focusing only on you and your team. With The Improv Mindset, we realize that there is something that can be far more powerful in either severely limiting or enabling your organization. Something that directly influences creative output and behavior: your corporate culture.

We believe culture is the lifeblood of your organization. It is the way you feel when you are at work. It can sometimes seem like a long-term employee who has incredible seniority, and it drives engagement and productivity like no other leader in the organization.

Corporate culture can be very difficult to pin down or define. Many of our clients can't even seem to agree on the *state* of their corporate culture. You can perform a survey with detailed questions about culture and get vastly different responses from everyone. And, no shocker here, the executive team's perspective will often look nothing like the general employee response to questions like:

- Do you feel trusted?

- Does management encourage creativity?

- If you fail, is the response a celebration or a nail in your coffin?

- Is your company efficient at running meetings?

- Do you have a voice?

- Do people listen to serve?

- Are your teams developed and supported by executive leadership?

- Are your company values just some words on a poster, or are they deeply engrained into how you do things?

You must at least address or acknowledge the culture you have before you can create, repair, or build a new one. If you ignore it or refuse to see it for what your employees truly feel it is, it will turn the head of the organization any way it wants.

For this reason, it's important to take a moment to dig a bit deeper into this whole concept of culture. We have a few clients who have done a culture analysis and brag about how "in tune" they are with their staff. Yet, when we work with them, we shed light on the fact that their assessment yields an awareness of larger issues.

And when those leaders have read the fine print, and discovered the areas of improvement within their organization, they are often unprepared to create a strategic approach to fix it.

A lot of that overwhelming paralysis in leaders stems from questions like: What makes a culture tick? What's it really made of? How can you change it?

Think of your culture as a complicated patchwork of different factors that are all stitched together. We think of those factors as inputs that look like this (Figure 26):

Figure 26: Inputs to Culture

History: Your history is not only how your organization was founded, it's also the ***myths and legends that surround it***. Tribal knowledge from senior employees, company mergers and acquisitions, and past leadership can all contribute to the history of an organization.

How You Do Things: This represents ***how your company gets work done***. Are managers expected to hold weekly status meetings? Do you have daily stand-up meetings? Is information accessible to all? How do your employees communicate? How do you manage your remote workforce? Do you use a project planning methodology? What technology do you use to enable collaboration? Do you celebrate both success AND failure? Do your employees engage in regular 360-degree micro-feedback?

Signs and Symbols: Signs and symbols exist throughout your organization. They include not only outwardly visible symbols (like your logo, or your Mission/Vision/Values statements), but also ***signs of power***, like corporate jets, expense accounts and weekly cocktail gatherings.

Hierarchy: As you might expect, your hierarchy represents ***how you are structured to get things done***. Who's in charge? Who reports to whom? Why is the reporting structure like it is? How important are titles? Most importantly, how does this affect the culture of the company?

Strategy and Financing: This represents things like budgeting, requests for money, and strategy definition and direction. Does anyone have more power in asking for and receiving budget funding? Who owns process creation and execution? Do people know HOW to get things done and are they allowed to collaborate in its development?

Decision Makers: The decision makers are not only those people who have more seniority in the hierarchy, they can also include informal decision makers who other employees turn to when they need answers. For example, the executive secretary that holds the keys for who can see the CEO has informal power within the company. Do you know who these key influencers are?

An Improv Mindset Culture

Where does The Improv Mindset fit into all of this? In companies that practice it, things like innovation and creativity influence everything, and vice versa (Figure 27).

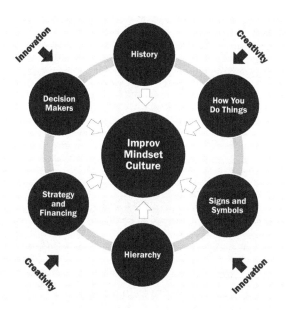

Figure 27: Inputs to an Improv Mindset Culture

Positive Characteristics of Creative or Innovative Companies

You probably know companies that have creative or innovative company cultures. They are usually on the top of the current business trend waves, never suffer a lack of possible recruits in the talent pool and enjoy incredible market share.

What do these companies have that gives them that competitive edge? Most certainly, a healthy culture. And, most likely that culture is tolerant of risk, open to new ideas and processes, and not afraid to evolve.

Look at the table that follows and take a few moments to list the positive characteristics of these kinds of companies (Figure 28).

Positive Characteristics of Creative or Innovative Companies	
1)	9)
2)	10)
3)	11)
4)	12)
5)	13)
6)	14)
7)	15)
8)	16)

Figure 28: Positive Characteristics of
Creative or Innovative Companies

This is a tool that we often use in our workshops, and it always amazes us how **consistent** the results are. Are any of the characteristics listed below similar to yours (Figure 29)?

Positive Characteristics of Innovative or Creative Companies	
1) Fun	9) Collaborative
2) People listen to new ideas	10) Like a start-up
3) Free food (yes, our clients actually say that)	11) Everybody is part of the team
4) High level of trust	12) Accessibility
5) Open	13) No fear
6) Fast-paced	14) Positive working environment
7) Forward thinking	15) Passionate
8) Allowed to fail	16) Learn quickly

Figure 29: Positive Characteristics of Creative or
Innovative Companies (examples)

Notice anything like the Four Rules of Improv we discussed in Section 3? Hint: Listening and Trust. There are also two other concepts that are closely related – Fun and Failure, both of which we'll explore a little later in this section.

Many successful companies weave the words and concepts around "Fun," "Trust," "Listening," and "Failure" into their core values, which helps to influence their corporate culture. Below are a few examples (Figure 30).

Company	*Published Core Values*
CarMax	Fun

Company	Published Core Values
	Communication Teamwork Respect
DaVita	Fun – We enjoy what we do. We know kidney dialysis is hard work; but even hard work can be fun. We take our jobs seriously, but we feel a fun environment delivers better care to our patients while creating a better work environment for our team-mates. We strive for excellence and we have fun. Team – One for All, and All for One! We work together, sharing a common purpose, a common culture and common goals. We genuinely care for and support, not only those to whom we provide care, but those with whom we work shoulder-to-shoulder. We work together to pursue achieving our Mission.
Zappos	Create Fun and a Little Weirdness Embrace and Drive Change Build Open and Honest Relationships with Communication Build a Positive Team and Family Spirit

Company	Published Core Values
Netflix	Curiosity (learn rapidly; seek to understand; broad knowledge) Innovation (re-conceptualize issues to discover practical solutions; challenge prevailing assumptions; create new ideas that prove useful) Courage (say what you think; make tough decisions; take smart risks; question actions inconsistent with their values)
Southwest Airlines	Fun-LUVing Attitude: • Have FUN • Don't take yourself too seriously • Maintain perspective (balance) • Celebrate successes • Enjoy your work • Be a passionate team player
The Motley Fool	Collaborate: Do great things together. Innovate: Search for a better solution. Then top it! Fun: Revel in your work.

Figure 30: Corporate Core Values (examples)

Let's be honest, though – The Improv Mindset culture is more than a series of 10 Core Values posters, or a plastic wallet card affixed to your security badge (though that's a start). It's a shared language and everyone's related behavior. For any culture to thrive, there must be a foundational structure to pave the way.

You must:

- Define it

- Teach it

- Practice it

- Reward it

This likely makes sense, though we find most of our client like proof. Researchers in Milan, Italy focused specifically on the climate for innovative teams in a variety of arts and performing organizations – that is, organizations that are required to be creative from the outset. These types of organizations have teams that are constantly building and collaborating on large projects.

The researchers found:

1) Focusing on the culture matters. Organizations that had better creative climates saw a direct correlation to the ability to improvise successfully.

2) There is a need to design and develop training initiatives foster improv.

3) Practice, practice, practice. This helps in improving existing attitudes toward dealing with ambiguity by encouraging improv. [37]

---

[37] (Magni & Palmi, 2017)

This sentiment is echoed in research that done in Melbourne, Australia at Monash University. The team focused on improvisation during safety-critical situations. Let's be honest, sometimes when you hear "safety critical" and "improv" in the same sentence, it seems counterintuitive. Researchers realized that little attention had been paid to looking at improv with regards to safety.

The team studied the incidents of outdoor lab activities – hiking, kayaking, white-water rafting, etc. They found that improvisation was successful for mitigating safety outcomes. As a matter of fact, the impact of improv was so profound they recommended that "organizations should embed provision for appropriate improvisation in their culture, policy and procedures, training and position descriptions."[38]

An organizational culture that is steeped in The Improv Mindset enables teams to "creatively adjust to change and to consistently move products and services out the door."[39]

Unilever is good corporate example. In 2013 they launched a program focused on growing leaders that would thrive in a world of constant change and turbulence. Their CEO Paul Polman believed improvisation ought to be used in tackling Unilever's biggest challenges. With their UL2020 program, they placed managers in teams of 5 that would innovate around big business challenges to generate breakthrough results. **The program generated millions of dollars in new revenue.**[40]

---

[38] (Trotter, Salmon, Goode, & Lenne, 2018)

[39] (Brown, 1998)

[40] (Samani & Thomas, 2017)

The point that we're making is that The Improv Mindset needs to be formalized in all directions in an organization to affect your culture and innovation capability. This will then lead to holistic organization learning, organizational structure and intuitive decision making.[41]

T *Improv Organization Questionnaire*

Now let's find out a little bit about YOUR corporate culture and its ability to tolerate this type of approach. This questionnaire is a useful tool for identifying how prepared your organization is for improvisation and creative thought (Figure 31).

Statement	Rank (1 = Low, 5 = High)
1) Your people have the skills they need to be creative in their work.	1 2 3 4 5
2) Teams are encouraged to form to address solving challenges, innovating new ideas, and collaborating on bold business strategies.	1 2 3 4 5
3) You encourage creative problem-solving through flexible processes.	1 2 3 4 5

---

[41] (Maimone & Sinclair, 2014)

Statement	Rank (1 = Low, 5 = High)
4) Managers do not take credit for other's ideas, rather they celebrate the success and creativity of their employees.	1 2 3 4 5
5) There are reward mechanisms for failure.	1 2 3 4 5
6) It's easy to get people together to solve a problem.	1 2 3 4 5
7) Failure is accepted.	1 2 3 4 5
8) People do not waste or disrespect new ideas.	1 2 3 4 5
9) Diversity of people is encouraged.	1 2 3 4 5
10) Corporate politics do not get in the way of a good idea.	1 2 3 4 5
11) New ideas are not judged harshly when they are shared.	1 2 3 4 5
12) Risk is encouraged.	1 2 3 4 5
13) There are reward mechanisms for new ideas.	1 2 3 4 5
14) You trust the people you work with.	1 2 3 4 5
15) When you have a new idea, you know where and how to share it.	1 2 3 4 5

Statement	Rank (1 = Low, 5 = High)
16) Your people stand behind decisions once they have been made.	1 2 3 4 5

Figure 31: Improv Organization Questionnaire[42]

Now go ahead and score the results. Take the corresponding value from your answers above and plug them into the next table (Figure 32).

Improv People		Processes for Improv	
Question	Scoring	Question	Scoring
1)		2)	
4)		3)	
6)		5)	
8)		7)	
9)		10)	
11)		12)	
14)		13)	
16)		15)	
Total		Total	

Figure 32: Improv Organization Questionnaire Scoring

---

[42] (McKeown, 2014)

This is a questionnaire we use with clients to understand what specific work they need to develop The Improv Mindset culture.

Regardless of the size of your organization, we'll typically start by conducting 15-20 interviews with mid- and upper-level leaders, using this tool as the conversation starter. The results can be quite enlightening (and sometimes, for senior leaders, quite surprising).

Take your results from above and plot them on our Improv Mindset Lifecycle Matrix below (Figure 33).

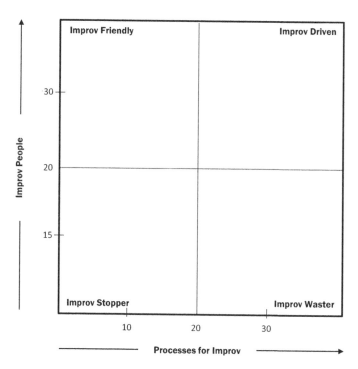

Figure 33: Improv Mindset Lifecycle Matrix

Where did you end up?

Improv Stopper: Your organization does not want or accept new ideas. New ways of thinking are frowned upon in deference to the thought "This is how we've always done it." Failure is never tolerated.

Improv Waster: Your organization is interested in new ideas and thinking differently, and yet corporate politics come into play every time there is a whisper of change. People are more interested in protecting themselves and their ideas than the company. As a result, only the people with the greatest political influence get a new idea pushed through.

Improv Friendly: Your organization has creative people who have great ideas, however no effective method for collecting and nurturing new approaches, let alone applying a different framework. There are few incentives for getting out there and trying something new. Therefore, unless someone has an idea that is a guaranteed win, ideas sit and wallow.

Improv Driven: Your organization has a framework for identifying and developing new ways of thinking. Anyone can share an idea or concept up and down the corporate chain and is rewarded for doing so. If the new idea fails, people do not place blame. Rather, they learn from the failure and move on to the next big idea.

As you might imagine, our clients rarely end up in the Improv Driven category. At an organizational level, we find that most businesses trend into the Improv Stopper category.

What can you do about it? Honestly, we've found it really depends on your organization. There is not a single prescription that applies to all companies, and it's important that the approach is tailored for your specific challenges, hierarchy, and organizational design. That said, there are some high-level issues that can be addressed for each category (Figure 34).

Lifecycle Category	Potential Questions
Improv Stopper	With Improv Stoppers, the first two things to address are: failure and trust. If you really want The Improv Mindset culture, **people must be allowed to fail.** This means that you need to spend time defining what failure really means and how you can begin to embrace it more. You must also identify why there are trust issues. Ask questions like: What happens when someone fails? How can we change the actions taken when people fail? What methods can we use to rebuild trust? Why are there trust issues?
Improv Waster	The hierarchy of an organization is often the culprit for Improv Wasters. You must first fix how the organization rewards and compensates new ideas and new ways of thinking. Ask questions like: What prevents people from bringing up ideas if they have them? What are the political barriers that keep the organization from exposing new ideas? Is there training that could provide people with new methods for collaboration?

Lifecycle Category	Potential Questions
Improv Friendly	Organizations that are Improv Friendly often require a more formal framework for how ideas get bubbled up to the surface. Ask questions like: What rewards are available for people who think of new ideas? Is there a budget devoted to innovation? If so, how is it spent? If not, is there a way to create one?
Improv Driven	Keep building upon what you're doing. Ask questions like: What's working and what isn't working? Is there additional training we can leverage? What else can we do to get people to think differently?

Figure 34: Questions for the Improv Lifecycle Roles

Not only can the Improv Organization Questionnaire be used to document current cultural impressions of your employees, it can also illuminate powerful disconnects between different levels of the organization.

For example, Figure 35 contains the combined results of two teams from one of our clients, a large software development company. The two teams were the Executive team (5 members) and the Software Development business unit (15 members).

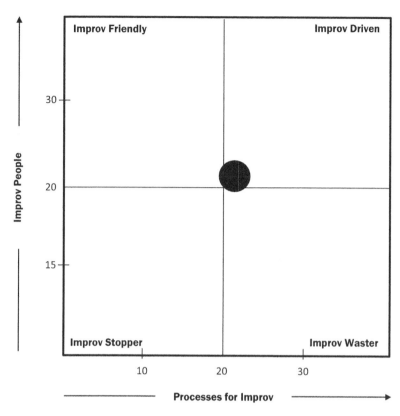

Figure 35: Improv Lifecycle Matrix - Software
Development Company

Doesn't look too bad, right? They've just crested the edge of the Improv Driven quadrant, and though they have room to grow, they're on the right path.

Now let's separate the results by functional group (Figure 36).

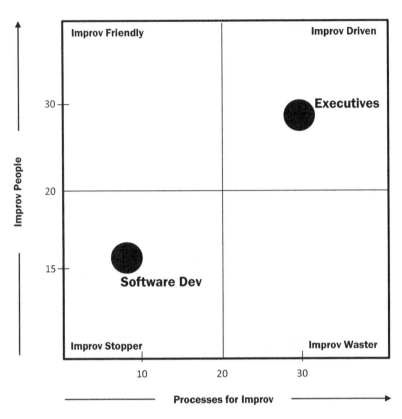

Figure 36: Improv Lifecycle Matrix - Software
Development Company (cont.)

Now there seems to be a different story. As we continued to work with this client, we found out that the Executive team was certain that their company was very progressive with new ideas, and, the Software Development team – the team actually implementing the work – did not feel the same. Further analysis uncovered that there were a couple of members of the Executive team who were exhibiting behavior that significantly undermined trust. Once these individuals started working through their trust issues, the Software Development team felt more inclined to participate – interesting stuff that was easily identified through the use of the tool.

Our experience begs the question, why do most organizations seem to trend toward Improv Stoppers? There can be lots of reasons, and we believe that it comes down to two things:

1) Most businesses don't want to deal with new ideas. They say they do, but they don't. They have no formal way to recognize or reward a new idea, and most people are comfortable doing exactly what they always do – the same old thing. Why? Because change hurts. Better to ignore change than accept it (this is due, in part, to the Judge).

2) No one can fail. If you fail, you're fired. Or something close to it.

How can we address this when we **know** companies need to be more agile? More open to change and new ideas? Our answer at a very basic level: Start by learning how to **improv**.

Researchers at American University of Beirut looked at the role of improv within construction companies. If you've ever done a remodel on your house, you know the necessity of being open to change – maybe those mahogany kitchen cabinets you ordered don't fit, or maybe you neglected to measure UNDERNEATH the refrigerator as part of the square footage for your new wood floors. At some point in a construction project, you'll find that things aren't exactly perfect. Enter improv.

The researchers found that, although a certain level of improv is expected out of workers, "companies should invest in training on the proper method."

Interestingly, they found that the blue-collar workers, that is the workers most likely to perform the actual work, were more likely to be comfortable improvising. Whereas, the white-collar workers did not have the same results.

"Improvisation is recommended as an essential type of decision-making...However, the benefits of improvisation will not be properly reaped unless companies make efforts to enhance the improvisation skills of their employees."[43]

Organizational Resilience & Creativity

Think back to the financial crisis of 2008. Those were scary times. People were losing their homes and their jobs, severe cutbacks were occurring up and down businesses, and the underbelly of the nation's problematic and complicated mortgage system was being exposed.

How were some organizations able to weather that blow, if not experience substantial growth, in the coming years?

The concept of "organizational resilience" is new in management research circles, and it's getting a lot of interest because of how quickly business conditions change. In order to survive, many organizations are finding themselves having to constantly pivot strategy and make do with less.

From 2008-2013 our financial institutions struggled. Researchers in Scandinavia looked at the performance of a bank that had startlingly better metrics than their peers during this time period – like 100% better (actual percentage).

---

[43] (Hamzeh, Alhussein, & Faek, 2018)

 Founded in 1871, Handelsbanken is a regional bank that targets the northern part of western Europe – Denmark, Norway, Sweden, Finland, the Netherlands, as well as branches in the UK. They are organized in a way that exemplifies The Improv Mindset culture.

1) They are a very flat organization. There are only 3 parts to their hierarchy: Corporate, Regional, and Branch. As a result, each employee is no more than two managers away from the CEO.

2) They put decisions in the hands of the people closest to the decision making – in their case, the Branch. There's no need to "run a problem up the chain" to get something done. The Branch is the most knowledgeable of local conditions. This enables agility at the bank level and the ability to improvise within the overall guiding principles.

3) The Branches are engaged and expected to provide feedback and input into future product design and new services.

Additionally, Handelbanken's corporate philosophy is structured to support the preference for cooperation, agility and improvisation, which includes:

- Decentralized structure

- Profitability *over* growth

- Customer-centric

- Product-related measures are forbidden – no compensation for selling or pushing a specific product

- Shared systems and corporate-wide visibility to reporting

From an employee perspective, they rotate employees laterally to numerous jobs, allowing broad experience, cross-training and a deep understanding of bank processes to propagate.

From a leadership perspective, here's something that's novel:

- Superiors are not allowed to criticize a decision that's already been made. Instead, they should offer active, close and knowledgeable support and dialogue. Imagine that in your company! [44]

The question is: How do you get it started when you don't have any of these frameworks in place? You start much like we've organized this book – at the individual (or the brain) level. From there you branch to the team and then to rest of the organization.

Let's look at another example that also comes from the northern part of Europe. Researchers in Finland looked at what they termed "Organizational Creativity (OC)," which represents the capacity that an organization empowers employees to take creative action that sustains **competitive advantage**. You might immediately be able to cite examples of companies that invest heavily in OC – Virgin, Amazon, Hulu, Apple, Google…you get the picture. In fact, that was what we talked about earlier when we asked you to think of qualities of creative companies.

The researchers understood that it's not just about generating good ideas, it's about holistic flexibility and agile capability. This allows individuals and groups to grasp a new idea and

---

[44] (Andersson, Caker, Tengblad, & Wicklegren, 2019)

helps companies **enact and implement new things**. It starts with individual creativity, which extends to collective creativity (or team creativity), which then extends to organizational creativity. You can think about it like a target (Figure 37), and the process works from the inside out; individual to organizational creativity.

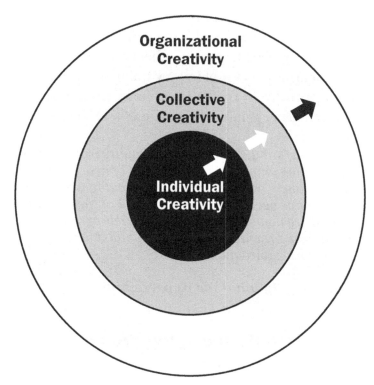

Figure 37: Creativity Target

The study focused on a Finnish municipality of 6,000 employees (as with any government entity, not necessarily what you would deem a "creative" organization). They spent 2.5 years analyzing the impact of running multiple groups through

3 sessions of improv training over 3 months. The workshops concentrated on increasing spontaneity, listening, trust, and group collaboration (sound familiar?).

They found that both individual creativity and collective creativity increased immediately. What about the organization? What about over the long haul of 2+ years?

The researchers discovered that **improvisation is "vital to fostering Organizational Creativity**, which is enabled by interacting individuals, and is only possible if they are able to openly shift their attention to others and stay actively focused on them. The power of improv training is that it creates and develops a collective potential of human resources, thereby achieving stronger cumulative capabilities and increasing OC."

> *Most importantly, "supporting creativity is not so much about having employees who are full of new ideas; it entails creating a social work environment in which people who perhaps never previously thought of themselves as creative are now empowered to use their creative abilities. Improv provides an excellent method for building such a work environment."* [45]

This is exactly what we're preaching.

Let's Celebrate the Thing We Fear Most: Failure

All the activities we've explored in this book, and many more we use with our clients, are steeped in the rules of Yes, and..., Listen with Intent to Serve, Support your Teammates AT ALL COSTS, and Trust your Instincts. As we hope you've learned,

---

[45] (Nisula & Kianto, 2018)

improv allows you to practice these rules at a very rapid pace while organically adjusting the architecture of your brain to be more responsive and more flexible. Additionally, improv allows you to **practice failure,** over and over and over again.

And in improv we don't just practice it, **we celebrate it.**

When was the last time you *celebrated* a failure at work? We're talking about the kind of failure where someone has a great idea and tries to implement it. And then it falls flat, or breaks something, or explodes! Our bet: it's never celebrated. Instead, we couch "failure" into meetings like "post-mortems" and "lessons learned." "How can we make sure that we never do this again?" we ask ourselves. The problem is, we don't **celebrate** it. It's a failure. And businesses *hate* failure.

Well, that's just ridiculous. And we want you to think so, too.

Let's start with a simple example – imagine you are a toddler learning how to walk. How many times do you think you will fall as you learn? A hundred times? A thousand times? Think about how crazy it would be to sit down and have a meeting every time it happened, being told that it could "never happen again," or that you needed to describe and document the lessons you've learned.

Come on. That would be a horrible way to learn. And we hope that most parents will just stand off to the side and laugh and clap and encourage you to try again. They are motivated to encourage you because it's a big deal!

If you want The Improv Mindset culture, failure must be treated as something AWESOME. After all, there is no success without it.

Now, by design, **improv gives you a way to practice failing**. Don't know how to do a Scottish accent? Well, you were just told that you're a Scottish shepherd, so step out there and be brave. You'll fail miserably, and we'll celebrate by laughing. By practicing failing through improv, we've found that you're better equipped to deal with "big" failure, and more likely to accept the risk of failing.

Have you ever seen the movie "Groundhog Day" with Bill Murray? It's a movie about a selfish, arrogant weatherman who is suddenly living the same day. After utilizing those days to his benefit and engaging in all sorts of crazy behavior, he begins to realize there may be a reason he is stuck in a "time loop." There is a scene toward the beginning of each day that the character relives where he steps into an icy pothole in the street. He does this several days in a row until one day, just as he is about to step in it, he stops, lifts his leg and steps OVER the hole. He learned from his previous "failure"!

If Edison's lab had a culture of reprimanding every failure, do you think he would have invented the lightbulb? What about the 39 failures before the invention of WD-40?[46] Or how about the 5,721 prototypes before Dyson completed his first cyclonic vacuum cleaner? That's not a made-up number, by the way. 5,721 prototypes! Celebrate failure – and in doing so you celebrate the effort of trying something new.

You may be wondering, "How do you **actually celebrate it?**"

There are several companies that have begun to spotlight their failures in fantastic ways. The company NerdWallet, for example, has a "Fail Wall" full of Post-it® notes bearing the failures of everyone, including the CEO. We believe that there's something refreshing about that. Actually *seeing* that you are

---

[46] (WD-40, 2014)

not alone in your failure, or that everyone fails no matter what their level, creates a diving board from which all employees can jump.

Tor Myhren, an ad agency executive, designed a Superbowl campaign for the Cadillac Escalade in the mid-2000's. It was such a colossal failure that it won several "Worst of" awards. This failure, however, did not keep him away from the world's largest advertising audience. The following year he created the E*Trade baby ad, which had a successful multi-year run. You may remember the ad campaign – it featured a baby seated at a computer. The baby would talk directly to the camera about how he was trading stocks on E*Trade. He'd say things like, "Boom! I just bought some stock." It was a tremendous success.

To help foster new ideas, Myhren started the "Heroic Failure Award," which he presents each year to the employee with the most epic fail. They get their name engraved on it, too![47]

The Indian company Tata Innovista has created the Dare to Try awards, which are given out for the best failures. The organization has a team that analyzes overall effort and potential impact, focusing on "what was learned from each failure" as the important component. The winners are recognized directly by the CEO in front of the entire company.[48]

We learn by failing.

If your employees aren't rewarded in some way for the crazy and "almost" ideas they bring to the table, **then why would they ever do it or keep doing it?** Most likely their ideas are not making it to a second thought because they keep remem-

---

[47] (Moran, 2014)

[48] (Sundheim, 2013)

bering what happened to that intern that sent a memo to everyone talking about her great idea – and then was never seen again. Finding time to weave this concept of celebrating failure into the very core of who you are as a business is key if you want The Improv Mindset culture.

However you celebrate failure in your organization, make sure it's BIG. You don't need a huge budget to do it, either. You just need to mark the occasion somehow, and make it matter. Every failure brings growth and learning. Period.

What are you SAYING?

Communication is essential to a healthy corporate culture. What kind of communication is exhibited in your teams? Do they text more than email? Do they email more than call? Do they call more than visit face-to-face? All methods of communication are important and have their place. Just remember that there is a "best" communication method for each situation and person, and your teams need to pick the right ones.

We have a good friend who consulted as a language translator for online information sharing. She told us that no one could communicate with one another in person. They were expected to Skype or use instant messenger, and that was it. She talked about how painful it was to be unable to get up and go to someone to ask a question or clarify something.

We're certain that the decision to be "technology-only" for communication was a rational one (most likely driven by cost). However, in our experience we've found that the absence of face-to-face time often leads to a lack of understanding and assumptions, and a deterioration of relationships between parties.

MIT's Human Dynamics Laboratory studied whether they were able to predict the success of a team by analyzing their communication patterns. They didn't analyze ***what*** the teams said to each other, just ***how*** they said what they said.

The researchers started with a group of call center agents and had them all wear electronic badges around their necks that recorded their physical interactions with coworkers, including things like: what direction they were facing, how long they spoke, and whether they nodded or used hand gestures. Based on the data, the researchers could then predict that Team A, for example, would be more successful at a particular task because their communications – both formal (in meetings) and informal (chatting around the water cooler) – involved engaged interactions that had a balance between talking and listening among team members. Again, the researchers didn't focus on the content of the conversation. Instead, they focused on some 100 different data points collected by each badge every minute.

The science behind this study is fascinating. From an evolutionary perspective, language is a relatively new process for the human brain. Underlying our verbal communication is a whole host of subtle cues that occur physically on an unconscious level – within our body language.

If we can understand how teams physically interact, then we can begin making changes that will have a significant improvement on team performance. And the financial gains from altering how teams interact can be staggering. One company is predicting a $15M increase in productivity due to increased efficiencies in team interactions.

So, at a high level, teams that perform well have members who:

- Talk to one another

- Are engaged when listening and have energetic gesture

- Listen almost the same amount as they talk

- Connect with the entire team, not just the person in charge[49]

Communication is often seen as a "soft science," and yet it isn't soft if we can increase profits by 15 million dollars through better team communication, is it? That's turning "soft" skills into hard results.

It's critical that we find language and tools that can positively change and improve team interactions. We need methods to increase listening and trust, which results in stronger teams. Methods like **improv.**

A New Leadership Competency

We can't really talk about culture without discussing leadership. We know that the concept of The Improv Mindset must be adopted at the executive level, who create the space for individual, team and organizational change. And, as we know all too well, leaders have a direct impact on performance. Successful organizations and teams are more likely to have leaders that:

- Are emotionally intelligent

- Use humor to diffuse conflict and motivate, even during times of intense pressure

---

[49] (Pentland, 2012)

- Delegate effectively and efficiently

- Foster open and clear communication

- Make things FUN[50]

Certainly, the Four Rules of Improv provide the opportunity to begin to flex those leadership muscles. Improv also teaches a leader something more important: ***agility***.

> *"An agile leader is one who embraces the change, adapts the trajectory, and uses change to achieve great things. In addition, an agile leader is better equipped to:*
>
> - *Deal with ambiguity and change*
>
> - *Make and implement decisions quickly*
>
> - *Think on his or her feet*
>
> - *Lead with confidence"*[51]

Francis Masson, Vice President of HR for Disney EMEA, notes that "this is about business outcomes, but it's also about 'learning by doing' and creating a new breed of talent who is resourceful, versatile, purpose driven, and stretched beyond their comfort zones."[52]

How can you practice being agile? Take a look at the next few exercises and get to work.

---

[50] (Sharma & Bhatnagar, 2017)

[51] (Trepanier & Nordgren, 2017)

[52] (Samani & Thomas, 2017)

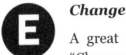

Change

A great exercise for practicing agility the game "Change." A facilitator will need a bell (or bell app on your smartphone).

The exercise starts with two people improvising a scene. After the first minute or so, the facilitator begins listening for a line in the scene that "needs to be rewritten." At that point, the facilitator rings the bell and says "Change."

The person speaking then must change the last line they just spoke to something else entirely. And the goal is to DRASTICALLY change the line, including the emotion and intent behind it.

The facilitator continues ringing the bell after each changed word or line until they hear something they like. Then, the scene continues from there. The facilitator can ring the bell at any time.

Here's an example of how a game of "Change" might go. Let's say that inspiration for the scene is "pineapple."

Scott: *See Janice? If you're really, really quiet, you can steal a pineapple from the farm.*

Janice: *Scott, this is not how I expected to spend my honeymoon.*

Scott: *C'mon. This is EXACTLY what we are supposed to be doing. Imagine how good a fresh pineapple is going to taste in your daiquiri.*

<Facilitator rings the bell>

Scott: *Imagine how we might use one of those fresh pineapples to exfoliate.*

\<ring\>

Scott: *Imagine what it must be like to work for Dole. I have a dream!*

\<ring\>

Scott: *Imagine if you just trusted me for ONCE. Is this how the entire marriage is going to be?*

Janice: *My father warned me about this.*

...and so on.

The advantage of this game is that it requires each player to be willing to jump from one idea to another, with incredible speed. As soon as the bell rings, you MUST change the last line. *And it has to be different.*

E Missing Letter

Another great exercise for practicing agility is the "Missing Letter" game. In this game, people are paired off and facing each other.

Each pair begins a two-person scene. After the first minute, the facilitator yells out a letter, for example the letter "O." The pair continues the two-person scene, but they cannot use the letter that was called out.

For example:

Matt: *Tom, can you help me with this rigging? I need to get on top of the roof.*

Tom: *Sure, Dad. I'll just put this ladder over to the side...*

<Facilitator yells out the letter "O">

Matt: *Yeah, sure. Just put it right there.*

Tom: *Did I just hear my maternal unit call me?* ← *(Notice that he didn't say "Mom" because the letter "O" is not allowed.)*

Matt: *Better stay here.* ← *(again, no "O")*

<Facilitator yells out the letter "S.">

Tom: *I'll be right here next to you, Dad.*

Matt: *Good, my progeny.*

And so on...

The facilitator can continue yelling out additional letters over time. The point is that the team is constantly working with the new challenge – bouncing from each letter and uncertain about what will come next, and the team is working TOGETHER. This is a challenging game that inevitably ends with the players frustrated and laughing because they struggle to not use the called-out letter.

Uncertainty is a fact of life. Why aren't we finding ways to be more comfortable with it? We MUST be agile in uncertain times.

> *"Uncertainty is challenging...Collaborative responses to uncertainty can create closer and more strategic relationships with customers and business partners...courageous spirits are often both more resilient and willing to*

be proactive. During periods of uncertainty, they gain competitive advantage."[53]

And, you guessed it, collaborative responses come while improvising.

Know When to Lead, Know When to Follow

Over the last several decades there has been a focus on Leadership within organizations and companies (and we mean Leadership with a capital "L"). What we find is that, overall, our clients mistake high performers for potential exceptional leaders. In our workshops we'll witness leaders who are really good at leading...or, at least, taking charge.

If we ask a leader to improv, it might be nerve-wracking for someone else, who isn't in management, to step out and start an activity with them. Yet, most of the members of an executive team seem to have no problem doing it. They lead things. Every day. That's their job.

Well, leading is only half the battle (actually a lot less than half, if you consider the statistic in the next sentence). You must have followers to lead, especially when "leaders contribute on the average no more than 20% to the success of most organizations." 20%![54] Therefore, we believe the more important topic lies in how organizations can breed cultures that encourage intuitive and talented *followers*. Improv is one of the few disciplines where everyone who participates has a

---

[53] (Coulson-Thomas, 2017)

[54] (Kelley, 1992)

chance both *to lead and to follow*, sometimes within seconds of each other (remember the core principle of "Yes, and..."). And you must practice doing both.

As we've come to find out, the follower/leader dynamic is directly related to trust. Think about it – it's almost impossible to really follow someone whom you don't trust to provide meaningful goals and productive direction. You might go through the motions, and in the back of your mind you're thinking, "This person doesn't know what they are doing." Additionally, it's impossible to lead effectively if you don't trust the people whom you're leading to follow through on your ideas.

MBA and executive training programs throughout the world emphasize the importance of leadership. Walk through the Business section of a bookstore and you'll see hundreds of books on it. We think there's been enough written about leadership. What about the other side of the coin? What about *follower*ship?

Coined by Robert Kelley in the early 1990's, followership is a fairly easy concept to grasp. It's "the ability to take direction well, to get in line behind a program, to be part of a team and to deliver on what is expected of you."[55] If you expound on the concepts of "Yes, and..." and "Support your Teammate at ALL costs," you begin to see how the rules of improv relate to making people *better leaders* in the context of decision-making and creative thought, *and also better followers* in terms of taking that thought and moving an idea forward.

Leadership and followership are reciprocally related, yet we spend most of our time worried about *how we lead*, even though most (if not all) of us are in a role where we report to

---

[55] (McCallum, 2013)

someone else. If you move up the entire leadership chain within an organization, you'll find that even the leadership team most likely reports to a board. Everyone must follow, at some point or another, and following can be very difficult.

T

What kind of follower are you?

Answer the questions below and we'll find out (Figure 38). *(Important note: This is a fairly comprehensive survey of 22 questions. It is necessary in order to get meaningful results.)*

Question	Rank (1 = Low, 5 = High)
1) Although I stay quiet, I often question the reasoning for a decision, rather than just doing what I'm told.	1 2 3 4 5
2) I am enthusiastic. And that enthusiasm has a positive impact on my team.	1 2 3 4 5
3) I am quickly successful with new jobs or tasks by defining and meeting metrics that are important to the leader.	1 2 3 4 5
4) I believe in the company's goals and priorities.	1 2 3 4 5
5) I can be successful in completing task assignments that don't have a lot of definition or are ambiguous.	1 2 3 4 5

Question	Rank (1 = Low, 5 = High)				
6) I can clearly articulate what I do well and what I don't do well.	1	2	3	4	5
7) I do whatever it takes to get the job done, even if I don't own it.	1	2	3	4	5
8) I enjoy playing the devil's advocate with my team and my leader.	1	2	3	4	5
9) I follow my own ethical standards over my company's.	1	2	3	4	5
10) I give my best ideas and highest performance.	1	2	3	4	5
11) I go above and beyond.	1	2	3	4	5
12) I identify and champion ideas that will impact the company.	1	2	3	4	5
13) I like to make my teammates look good, even without getting any credit.	1	2	3	4	5
14) I set priorities and decide what's most important to achieve my team's goals.	1	2	3	4	5
15) I speak my mind on important issues, even though it might cause conflict with the team or with my leader.	1	2	3	4	5
16) I take the initiative to solve tough problems within the company.	1	2	3	4	5

Question	Rank (1 = Low, 5 = High)				
17) I understand what is expected of me from my leader.	1	2	3	4	5
18) I work to become more valuable to the company by increasing my competence in mission-critical activities.	1	2	3	4	5
19) If someone asks me to change, I am more likely to say "Yes" rather than "No."	1	2	3	4	5
20) My job is either professionally or personally fulfilling.	1	2	3	4	5
21) Once a decision is made, I stand behind it 100% (even though I may have disagreed with the idea).	1	2	3	4	5
22) I get excited by learning new things.	1	2	3	4	5

Figure 38: Adapted from R.E. Kelley's Followership Survey[56]

Score your results in the table below by taking the corresponding value from your answers above and plugging them in (Figure 39).

Scoring:

---

[56] (Favara Jr., 2009)

Thinking on your Own		Engaged in the Organization	
Question	Scoring	Question	Scoring
1)		2)	
6)		3)	
8)		4)	
9)		5)	
12)		7)	
14)		10)	
15)		11)	
16)		13)	
19)		17)	
20)		18)	
22)		21)	
Total		Total	

Figure 39: Followership Survey Scoring

Take the totals and plug them in the 4x4 box in Figure 40.

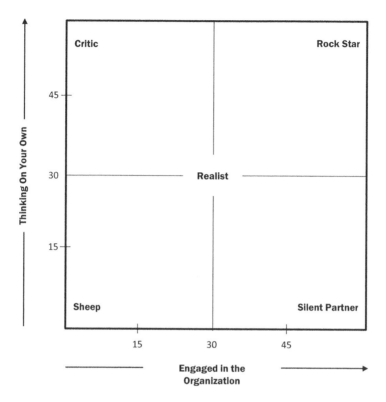

Figure 40: Followership Survey Graph

Where'd you end up?

Rock Star: The Rock Star is the person you want on your team or the person you want to be. They provide value and self-management, and they can see how they fit into the overall picture of the organization. They adapt quickly and efficiently and have a personal motivation to be good at their job.

- *What you should do if you're a Rock Star:* If you're a Rock Star – Congratulations! We also remind you to not get complacent. Keep challenging the status quo, learning new things, and identifying methods to make you and the company better. Look for training opportunities to learn the latest in your field. Develop content and speak at a conference.

- *What you should do if you have Rock Stars on your team:* The biggest challenge with Rock Stars is that they can get bored easily. Continue to keep them engaged by involving them in decision-making and encouraging them to bring new ideas to the table. Train them on cutting edge technologies and new methods of doing things.

Critic: Though the Critic does a good job thinking of new ideas, they are much more comfortable criticizing the ideas of others than coming up with any of their own. They feel alienated, like no one understands them, and they revert to "the old ways are better" when a new idea comes up that is not theirs. As a result, they play a challenging role in an organization.

- *What you should do if you're a Critic:* Ask yourself: "Why?" There can be many reasons – baggage from a layoff, bad experiences with current leadership, not getting recognized when you felt you should have been, or just plain old fear of change. Document your reasons. Next ask yourself "What behavior would need to be exhibited for me to trust those around me?" *(probably many of the behaviors described in this book).* Then, begin engaging in activities that encourage others to demonstrate those behaviors. You start by addressing trust first. What if it's your boss you don't trust? Ah, that's a lot more complicated, but you can start with something simple: Talk to them. See if you can find common ground and work from there.

- *What you should do if you have Critics on your team:* Focus on trust. Critics typically want to participate, and they don't feel that they can for fear of reprisal. Without first finding ways to build a framework for trust, critics will never become Rock Stars. And regardless of what you do, they will most likely fight any attempt to move them. Just keep providing proof that trust matters. Follow through on your commitments and demonstrate the behavior you expect.

Sheep: The Sheep is the person who is neither engaged nor participating. They require a leader for everything. Think of the Sheep like the production line factory workers of the early 1900's. They are disinterested in establishing direction or providing input to new ideas.

- *What you should do if you're a Sheep:* You'll need a major overhaul of how you approach new thoughts for you to move toward being a Rock Star. Start finding ways to think and talk about new ideas, such as a weekly lunch or coffee where you ask people what else you could be doing. Nurture any new idea you have and run it by your boss. Find ways to participate in the decisions being made around you.

- *What you should do if you have Sheep on your team:* You're going to need a big change to your culture if you want to move Sheep into different categories. Start by identifying the culture you want and involve the Sheep from the very beginning. Set expectations for behavior and follow through. Provide training on new idea development and trust.

Silent Partner: The Silent Partner is a person who is invested and engaged, and likely has no opportunity to express those thoughts. They rely completely on the leadership to make decisions and come up with ideas; otherwise they're comfortable keeping their head down and doing their job.

What you should do if you're a Silent Partner: It's understandable that you trust the leaders to lead and make all the decisions, and we know that you have good ideas that you're keeping under wraps. Read books on best practices for your industry or function. Start an "idea lounge" where you talk about challenges with your peers. Start a book club and ask your leaders to participate. Go to conferences. Trust the ideas you DO have and find moments to share them.

What you should do if you have Silent Partners on your team: Sometimes the reason they are silent is that no one has ASKED them how they feel or what they want. Silent Partners need to be encouraged to share and imagine a new process or future. Ask your people what motivates them, then design incentives for new ideas that speak to those motivations. Provide training. Create an innovation space (see Innovation Room later in the section). Encourage employees to devote part of their workday to expanding their horizons.

Realist: Ah, the most common role. The Realist doesn't want to rock the boat. They are pragmatic. They might often utter the phrases, "I've seen this before," or "What's in it for me?" They like to shoot down ideas or changes based on the

fact that "they know better." They are engaged in the organization to a point yet prefer that no one make any drastic changes.
They're like guard dogs – constantly ready for a fight should
someone dare to bring a new idea up.

- *What you should do if you're a Realist:* You need to
  look inwardly and determine WHY you are so reti-
  cent to change. Trust tends to be the issue, as is your
  personal experience. You should find ways to disrupt
  your current thinking at the same time as developing
  trust (maybe improv?). Read through the approaches for the Critic and the Silent Partner for
  ideas. Try to open your eyes to the possibility of
  change and the "other" side of the coin.

- *What you should do if you have Realists on your
  team:* The Realists lack a willingness to "go along".
  They don't like change. You need to involve Realists
  at the inception of any discussion about innovation,
  and then document every success and every failure.
  Seek their expertise and leverage them as key influencers. Trust us, Realists know when something
  works, and something doesn't, so they need constant
  inspiration to believe differently. Provide training
  and methods for deepening trust. Incentivize new
  ideas (see Incentives later in this section).

We often use this tool as part of a large-scale culture analysis
to help gauge the temperature of a team or organization. First,
it's useful to get an understanding about **how** you are "showing
up," even though you may already be aware of how comfortable
you are in sharing or hearing new ideas, going along with the
norm, or trying different ways of doing things.

Second, if you anonymously survey an entire group and plot the results, you get a sense of what you're up against when implementing or shifting to The Improv Mindset. Sure, you may feel you inherently *know* which person is engaged and which is not, and yet this can be a powerful visual aid to illustrate the challenges you might face. You may end up with results that you didn't expect!

See Figure 41 for results from one of our clients.

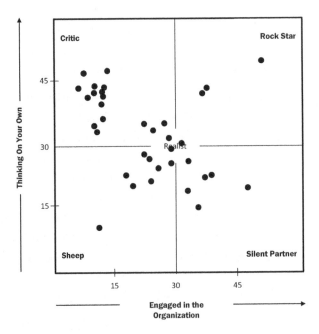

Figure 41: Followership Survey Graph (example)

Notice any concerns or trends? How about that cluster of Critics? These are people who know in their bones that they have good ideas, *and* they have deep-seeded mistrust for the organization. Problem? Absolutely – and now you know that you need to address trust issues swiftly.

Remember: Knowing how to lead is critical to your organization. Knowing how you and your people *follow* is critical to an organization's success.

There's another vital reason for understanding followership: people who have higher followership scores have better job performance and higher job satisfaction. A study out of Northcentral University analyzed 131 employees of an automotive engineering and manufacturing plant. As part of the study, the employees were asked to complete a survey similar to the one you just did. Additionally, each manager was asked to rate the performance of the employees. The study found that the people who were in the Rock Star quadrant performed better and were happier employees.[57] So, if you increase your followership scores, you will most likely see increased job performance and satisfaction.

So how does the leadership/followership dynamic fit into improv? What's the relationship? Recall what we mentioned in the beginning of this section: you are required to both lead and follow in improv, sometimes within a matter of seconds. And you need to practice both.

Just like endlessly cutting onions as an Iron Chef or passing the puck back and forth in hockey, improv is a method for practicing leading and following in the same exercise, which makes you more prepared for when you actually have to do it in the real world. Because of this, you naturally increase trust and creativity as well.

---

[57] (Favara Jr., 2009)

How does improv prepare participants for leadership AND followership? Well, there are three "roles" in improv: the Initiator, the Reactor, and the Back Foot. Each role is an important component of an improv exercise (Figure 42).

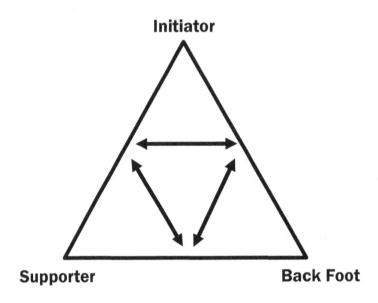

Figure 42: Improv Roles Pyramid

- The ***Initiator*** is the brave soul who steps out with an idea. They are the ones who commit to making a choice and going with it, no matter what.

- The ***Supporter*** is the teammate who comes in almost immediately to support whatever (and we mean *whatever*) the Initiator has decided to do. Remember the rule: Support your Teammates AT ALL COSTS.

- The ***Back Foot*** is any other team member listening for whatever support might be required.

Here's an improv example. Let's say that two women, Lisa and Elena, are on stage getting ready to play a two-person scene. The moderator asks for an idea to get them started (in improv we call this a "give" and it is part of the unpredictability of improv – you never know what you're going to get). The audience screams out a bunch of ideas and the moderator chooses the idea "bus stop." So, the idea, or the "give," for the exercise is "bus stop." That's all Lisa and Elena get. They now incorporate "bus stop" into the exercise.

The ***Initiator*** is the first person motivated who steps out to start the exercise. In this case, let's imagine that Lisa steps forward and starts nervously looking up and down the street, saying "I can't believe it's late. My boss is going to kill me." After several seconds or two she screams, "C'mon. Where is that bus?!"

Realizing that the scene now needs a bus (and doing a little "Yes, and...") the ***Supporter*** (Elena) immediately steps off to the side and pretends to be a bus driver driving a bus. She pulls up, stops the bus, and says, "Sorry I'm late. I hit a parked car, but nobody saw me."

As you might expect, the exercise can go anywhere from there.

Where does the ***Back Foot*** fit in and who does it? People who play the Back Foot are there to provide anything the exercise requires, without taking away or detracting from it. In this case, a couple of Back Feet might step forward and pretend to be other people at the bus stop, or people on the bus itself. They add character and depth to the exercise. They are there to support the team.

It looks like this (Figure 43):

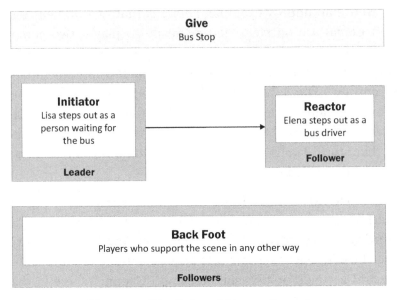

Figure 43: The Roles of Improv Layout

You should be, know and experience ALL those things. As leaders and teammates, if you are always driving it's a dictatorship. If you are always supporting, there's no chance for growth. If you are waiting in the wings to be called upon, you will never feel the exhilaration of being the driver.

Great leaders know this. They lead and inspire others to lead. They know when to support an idea and when to be the champion for its momentum. They also know when to lay low and help with the lift as needed. If you have employees who are uncomfortable with ambiguity, that is normal. Improv forces us to "play" within that pool.

Personality Assessments

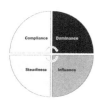

Influencing your corporate culture takes hard work and discipline. It also takes people…who can occasionally be unpredictable. So, it stands to reason that the more information you can gather about your people, the better.

Enter the Personality Assessment (PA). The PA is another great way to give you and your teams a common vocabulary, and to identify preferred and non-preferred methods of communication. It always makes us chuckle a little when we suggest doing this with our clients. The consistent gut response seems to be "well we did that with a consulting company, and we all know what we are."

Our questions:

- What did you **do** with the information after you were given the results?

- Do you make good use of the assessment in how you **relate** to your co-workers?

It's good to know the personalities of you and your team, and they are more successful when their members are self-aware.

There are lots of assessments out there (Myers Briggs, Insights, Hermann Brain Dominance, etc.). We like the **DISC Assessment** because it's been around for many years, is widely available, and has much information written about it. The DISC Assessment was created by Dr. William Marston, whose research determined that your behavior could be plotted into four quadrants. Each of those quadrants has associated personality descriptions.

More importantly, you can map those quadrants to the roles in improv (Initiator, Reactor, Back Foot). Why does that matter? Remember in the first section we discussed brain plasticity and making your brain more flexible? This is done not only by trying new things, but also by trying things that make you (and your brain) uncomfortable – like brushing your teeth with your non-dominant hand. We use the DISC Assessment to identify where people tend to be more comfortable in improv, then design exercises that force them into uncomfortable places (Figure 44).

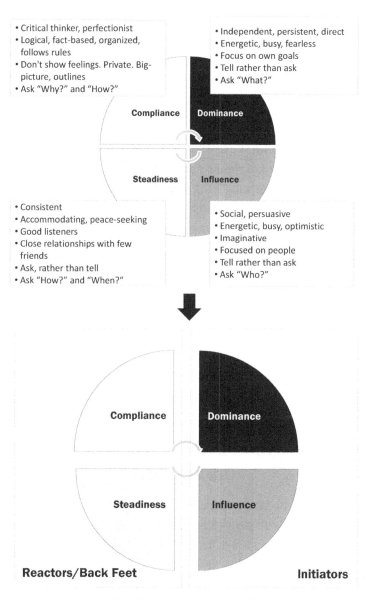

- Critical thinker, perfectionist
- Logical, fact-based, organized, follows rules
- Don't show feelings. Private. Big-picture, outlines
- Ask "Why?" and "How?"

- Independent, persistent, direct
- Energetic, busy, fearless
- Focus on own goals
- Tell rather than ask
- Ask "What?"

Compliance   **Dominance**

Steadiness   **Influence**

- Consistent
- Accommodating, peace-seeking
- Good listeners
- Close relationships with few friends
- Ask, rather than tell
- Ask "How?" and "When?"

- Social, persuasive
- Energetic, busy, optimistic
- Imaginative
- Focused on people
- Tell rather than ask
- Ask "Who?"

Compliance   **Dominance**

Steadiness   **Influence**

Reactors/Back Feet   **Initiators**

Figure 44: DISC Assessment Model Compared
to the Roles of Improv

For example, in our experience, psychiatrists and IT Engineers seem to fall into the Compliance category, whereas Marketers identify with Dominance and Influence. By continually pushing teams out of their comfort zone and putting them in positions to work within the opposite side of their personality preference, the brain begins to make new connections and ultimately encourages new behaviors.

One caveat about Personality Assessments – they are not the final word. We've seen organizations that use it as another way to label each other. "Oh, you're an 'Influencer' and I'm a 'Compliant' – therefore I despise you." Or, "You're a 'Dominant,' therefore you're just going to walk all over me."

It's imperative that companies shift the way that they use this information within their organizations. They can and must be leveraged to connect individuals, diversify teams, and increase Emotional Intelligence within the business as a whole. Having robust knowledge about the way a co-worker approaches conflict, prefers to receive information, and generally "shows up" can be a valuable tool in solving problems and solidifying internal relationships.

Your Employees Don't Trust Your Company (by default)

Be ready – no matter what change your company is trying to implement, your people aren't going to trust it. In general, change breaks down trust. In a study at Baylor University, subjects were analyzed using an fMRI.

> *"...during the scan, research subjects read short vignettes. Some were about objects, such as a piece of fruit or ironing board, while other stories told of people or*

corporations performing pro-social actions (e.g., donating to charity), anti-social actions (e.g., lying or breaking the law), or neutral actions (e.g., buying a printer)."[58]

As one might expect, specific areas of the brain became active when participants were asked about objects vs. people. However, the areas of social reasoning that activated during questions about people ***also engaged when asked about companies***.

What does this mean? It means that we interact with companies ***as if they are human beings***. They aren't the static, monolithic institutions that we write about in business magazines. According to our brains, they are living, breathing entities, and this means that they are more likely to protect and keep what has worked in the past rather than adopting new approaches.

There's likely a component in evolution as to why we think this way: businesses haven't been around that long. Quite possibly, because we are part of the whole of this "thing", we feel responsible and protective of it. Our brain connects to it the best way it knows how.

Also, companies have one more thing against them – our brain is negatively biased toward their actions. Through the study, the researchers found that the brain is telling us that we should be suspicious of the actions of a company just like we should be suspicious of a stranger on a dark street.[59] Without any proof or reasoning!

We all know that humans fear change. Add a layer of suspicion onto any change in business and things get more difficult.

---

[58] (Guittierez, 2014)

[59] (Plitt, Savjani, Savjani, & Eagleman, 2015)

The new buzzwords of today's businesses like innovation, creativity, and flexibility all require openness to change on a very basic level.

How do you make people better at change? More comfortable in ambiguity? You engage them in creating, adopting and implementing it. You create space to teach, demonstrate, and perform it. You collaborate and practice it in a safe environment where there are clear rules and expectations of behavior.

You *improv*. And you *change*.

The Improv Mindset Contract

Creating The Improv Mindset culture takes work and commitment. We often have clients who call us and ask, "Can't you just get this done in a couple of days? Or a week?" Our answer: Absolutely not.

How do you get *started* in the effort to change organizational culture?

We thought you would never ask. First, you need rules – rules that define how you expect the people in your organization to behave. A contract, if you will. Start with the Four Rules of Improv from Section 3.

This is only the beginning. We strongly recommend crafting a total of 10 rules that define this new behavior (the number 10 has always seemed to resonate with our clients). Here's an example:

The Improv Mindset Contract

1) Say "Yes, and..." before saying "No."

2) Balance listening with the intent to serve with speaking.

3) Trust your instincts.

4) Embrace failure.

5) Support your teammates (at all costs!).

6) Start meetings on time. End meetings on time.

7) Value diversity of opinions and skills.

8) If you hit a roadblock with the team, stop and laugh. Then try again.

9) Get behind decisions, even if you initially disagreed with them.

10) Fun above all.

Don't spend hours crafting and rewording. Keep it simple so that everyone can understand it. Also consider WHO helps with the development of these rules. Engaging the right key influencers and champions within your company can ease future adoption and build trust among peers.

Next, make sure everyone understands the rules of the contract. You can't just march out and say "Here's how we're going to behave going forward" without giving context for why you're changing, why it's important, and what the expectations are. Once people understand "why" it's important, then it's much easier to get them to support the idea and get your entire team or organization behind the rules.

As we mentioned earlier in this section, your teams will be immediately skeptical of anything new that your organization is trying. Even if it's the right decision, the best choice, and the most needed change – their brains will fight it. Additionally, they might remember what came down the pipeline before, and how things "fizzled out," failed or lost momentum. So, don't underestimate the challenge of creating a strategy to move everyone.

It will also be necessary to determine what happens when someone "breaches" the contract. Holding people accountable is critical. Otherwise, people will just continue their same old behavior. An approach many clients of ours use is giving their employees permission to state or "call out" when someone isn't behaving according to the contract. Anyone, from administrative assistant to CEO, can call out others without retribution. This behavior takes a tremendous amount of trust.

One thing is certain: Cultural changes won't stick unless the entire team or entire organization is *all in.*

For example, one COO we worked with took the "Start meetings on time. End meetings on time" from The Improv Mindset Contract to the extreme. If you didn't start within two minutes of the starting time, followed by clearly stating an agenda, other people were permitted to get up and leave. She then made a powerful step toward correcting behavior by testing it herself. She called a meeting with 20 or so employees. After five minutes of pretending to answer emails and work on her phone she stated, "I've violated our contract. I haven't started the meeting, nor have I said what we're going to do. And you're still here. This meeting is over."

It can't be overstated the importance of trust once these rules are established and everyone has committed to the contract. The average employee would never have the courage to get up from their chair and leave a meeting if their manager hadn't stated the agenda in a timely manner. This is why these changes need to be championed fiercely by top executives and practiced religiously.

One other point about changing meetings. If there are people who always start their meetings on time, everyone knows this and is aware of the need to be there. If they are always late or wait for people to join in person or on a call, then it is understood as acceptable. As consistent practice of these rules happen, behavior **will** change.

Approaches to Changing Culture

Other client approaches to changing culture have included:

- Everyone at the table yells "No" when someone says "No" or "Yes, BUT..." The offenders quickly become aware of when they are not supporting the "Yes, and..." rule.

- Require every meeting to begin with a fun activity. Laughter is encouraged before the meeting starts to create a foundation of levity and to break the ice.

- Use the Five Second Rule (see Section 3) as a meeting facilitation approach. No matter what is said, no one can respond without first waiting 5 seconds (or any number of seconds you define).

- Throw a party at the end of each month to celebrate the adoption of the new rules.

Lastly, everyone needs to be reminded of The Improv Mindset contract. Place it in meeting rooms. Put it up on people's doors. Make it a visible and physical representation of your culture. Celebrate the intention of shifting your culture and everyone's role in doing so.

The Idea Pipeline

As you begin to tap into the collective knowledge of your employees and work to create an Improv Mindset culture, new ideas will (hopefully) start coming your way. What's the best way to reward those ideas? How can you make sure that you keep them coming, and keep them coming consistently?

There's been a lot of debate within companies over the last few years – should you give one giant prize like Google or 3M? A big payoff to motivate your employees? Or, maybe it's better if you give small prizes. Will that mean that your employees won't be as interested, though?

A recent study from the University of Southern Denmark analyzed both the big and small prize approaches. Interestingly, they found that big rewards can have a negative impact. Think about it like this – you're going to give, say, $100,000 to the team that comes up with the best way to solve what we'll call "Problem X." This presents a challenge – when you have a big reward, many people will want to solve it. So, you'll get a LOT of solutions.

This is good, right? Actually, no. The researchers found that you'll most likely end up with an idea pipeline bottleneck. There will be many good, even great, ideas among the glut of submissions, and you'll have so many that you won't be able to go through them in a timely fashion.

According to the study, a better approach is to focus on smaller rewards, such as 5-15% of an idea's value. This in turn allows for a more consistent idea pipeline because not everyone and their dog are trying to get the big reward.[60]

By the way, this may seem to fly in the face of some of the earlier talk of "more ideas = more ideas of value." It doesn't. What we are talking about here is the INCENTIVE piece that drives your employees to submit those ideas. If you set the prize too high, folks have an instant need to submit every idea to "win." At that point, innovation becomes about "winning" and not about solving problems. Subtle though it might be, it is still an important distinction.

Regardless of the approach, one thing is clear: people need time to think about BIG innovations. You can't expect your employees to fit innovative thought and research into their day without making room for it. Many of our clients are under the impression that "OK, you've learned about the importance of innovation...now go and innovate," without adjusting workloads to allow for it. We cannot stress this enough: If you want people to be inspired to think differently, you need to give them time (and money) to do so.

There are many examples of forward-thinking companies (including Google, 3M, and Arrow) that allow their employees to devote 15-20% of their time to a project they want to work on. Menlo Innovations plans for every employee to have a 32-hour work week, with the remaining 8 hours devoted to training, exploration, and idea generation.

Remember: if you're going to change your culture, you must commit to a new way of doing things. This includes **changing how your employees are spending their time** in order

---

[60] (Baumann & Stieglitz, 2014)

to make room for innovative thought. You can start by scaling back on low-value meetings and status reports. We know you have them.

You also need to identify your feedback tool for collecting new ideas. Look at things like:

- Employee suggestion box

- Idea management software (though you must address process first and not just expect that the technology will be your "solution")

- Hackathons – bring all business analysts and programmers together to solve a specific problem. Spend one or two days programming a solution

- Innovation days – bring everyone together to solve a specific problem. Reward the solution!

Finally...FUN and LAUGHTER!

As promised, we want to end this section with some thoughts on FUN.

Two of the most important byproducts of improv are fun and laughter, and they go hand-in-hand with each other. If you're having fun, you're most likely laughing, and vice versa.

The good news is that **laughing makes you feel good** – and not just your state of mind, laughing actually **improves the physical state of your body**. There have been numerous studies over the last 15 years that found laughing:

- Provides a 27% increase in beta-endorphins, the body's natural pain killer

- Lowers cortisol, a stress-related hormone

- Dilates the blood vessels to increase blood flow

- Increases immune system antibodies[61]

Researchers believe that "laughter evolved as an alternative mechanism for reinforcing social bonds in groups beyond those that can be maintained by primates."[62] Additionally, "this mechanism is mediated by **opioid release** in a network anchored to the brain structures mentioned above."[63]

Yep, our brain is producing opioids when we laugh.

In our experience, laughter and fun in the workplace are far less common than they should be. Yet many people inherently understand that there is a relationship between laughter and a good place to work (Figure 45).

---

[61] (Buck, 2008)

[62] (Manninnen, et al., 2017)

[63] (Caruana, 2017)

Figure 45: Impact of a Fun Working Environment

Why don't companies do more about this? We find many of our clients *know* that fun, laughter and humor are important, yet there seems to be a prevailing belief that it's just not appropriate. As if there's a connotation to laughter that you're goofing off, and work is **SERIOUS** business. Lately, cutting-edge science and research is proving that laughter is a critical part of team success.

At its core, laughter is largely about relationships. Think about the number of times you are alone in front of the TV and the number of times you laugh while you're sitting there. Now compare that to when you are in a social situation. You will laugh 30 times more in a group than you will by yourself![64] It makes sense, then, that there's a deep *social* context to laughter – you engage in it more when you are in a group.

Also, studies show that good leaders use considerably more humor than bad leaders do. And 97% of the firm Robert Half International feel managers need to have a sense of humor as it creates a better work climate and improves relationships.[65]

So, how does this apply to teams at work? Researchers at the University of Amsterdam completed a two-year study that analyzed the relationship between humor in teams and their associated performance. This is one of the main reasons we started our company – we wanted to help other businesses understand when teams laugh together they *stay* together.

The researchers recorded the behavior of 54 teams (352 people) over the course of the two years. First, they found that teams using humor laugh regularly together and **produce more and have better outcomes**. Second, they determined that laughter was a powerful way of setting up a creative task, and subsequently the teams that laughed together while they were brainstorming **had more ideas**.[66] That's exciting stuff!

We've had a similar experience with our clients. We commonly use the Alternate Uses Test (remember the Paperclip Test in Section 1?) as a method of measuring idea generation before and after our workshops. At the end of our workshops we've seen an increase across teams as high as 81%, with some individuals having as high as a 200% increase! We know that

---

[64] (Buck, 2008)

[65] (Gopalkrishnan, 2017)

[66] (Lehmann-Willenbrock & Allen, 2014)

some of this is related to The Improv Mindset – and along with that disruption comes laughter, fun and humor.

Additionally, as researchers at Istanbul Commerce University found, for a company to be successful in this ever-changing business world, it is important to cultivate a corporate climate that encourages both freedom and flexibility, that fosters humor as well as creativity, and reinforces the relationship between humor and creativity.[67]

Improv does all those things.

---

[67] (Kocak, 2018)

Section 5
The Improv Mindset
4i Methodology

"I can't understand why people are frightened of new ideas. I'm frightened of the old ones."

— John Cage

The last area we're going to explore is The Improv Mindset 4i Methodology. If you think of the structure of this book as a pyramid, we've been focusing on each concept in order, starting with your brain (Figure 46).

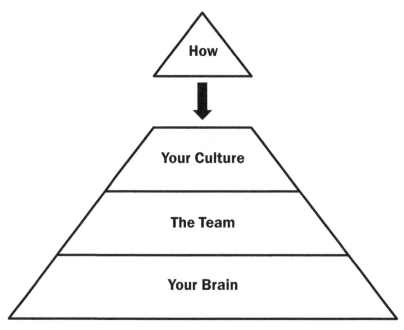

Figure 46: The Improv Mindset Pyramid

It's not a bad idea to think about The Improv Mindset process in this order. Only after you've addressed your brain, your team, and organizational culture should you layer on a formal methodology for people to follow.

However, we find organizations do just the opposite – they put methodology at the bottom of the pyramid and promptly ignore the rest of the levels, ***expecting that the methodology will fix everything***. This approach has challenges. If you want the methodology to stick, you must begin by addressing core behaviors – because if you don't, you'll have a great methodology with lots of pretty tools and no one using them. You can't build the rocket ship and then just expect everyone to get on board. Remember: with The Improv Mindset you change your BRAIN and it will change your BUSINESS.

This doesn't mean that you can't introduce a methodology for The Improv Mindset early on. As a matter of fact, having a general understanding can help a newly formed team prioritize a goal. Just do it AFTER you've introduced and practiced rules like: Yes, and..., Listen with Intent to Serve, Support your Teammates AT ALL COSTS, and Trust your Instincts.

Having studied various methodologies introduced over the last 50 years (from 1950's Osborn and Parnes creative problem-solving to TRIZ to OODA Loops to Design Thinking), we find that they all have similar structure.

Through our research and practical experience, we've developed The Improv Mindset 4i Methodology. It looks like this (Figure 47).

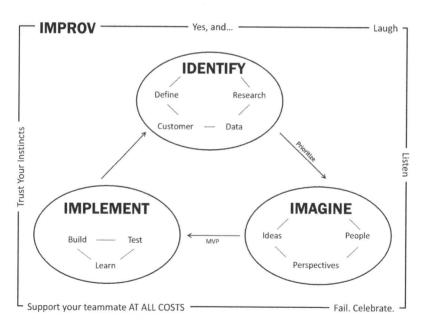

Figure 47: The Improv Mindset 4i Methodology

Let's briefly explore each stage of the methodology and how each piece fits into the overall process.

Improv

You'll notice right away that IMPROV is the overarching perimeter or "glue" in this methodology. You can't expect people to come together and begin working as a team without first giving them a chance to BE a team. Think about the last meeting you were in. Did you warm up the brain? Did you laugh? Or did you just sit around the table listening to someone talk?

We suspect we know the answer.

Improv gives teams the rules and vocabulary that set the framework for working and creating together – things that need to be practiced and studied (just like a basketball or hockey team). Improv puts you and your teams into the **mindset** to be radical, disruptive, and creative, which forces your team to focus on the core RULES:

- Yes, and...

- Listen with Intent to Serve

- Support your Teammates AT ALL COSTS

- Trust your Instincts

As well as:

- Laugh

- Fail

- Succeed

- Celebrate

Identify

The next stage is to IDENTIFY the problem or challenge you want to work on. You may already know what it is. You may not. Regardless, the steps are the same.

First, identify the question or problem you want to focus on. The question can be broad or specific, depending on your goals. Here are some examples from our clients:

- Why are we getting complaints about our new software?

- Why does IT have a bad reputation in the organization?

- How can we increase sales without adding headcount?

- What are the challenges with communication between our doctors and the staff?

- How can we provide consistent power throughout the design process?

Or, you can have a completely different goal and ask the question: "What's our next big invention?"

Second, bring a group together offsite and **detail** the reasons why a problem is occurring. Use sticky notes and have team members write down why a problem could be happening. There's a change management component to this step – one goal is to get everyone on board with the problem, and another goal is to make sure people agree it should be solved.

Third, go and gather **data** about your problem or challenge. Gather data any way you can. Talk to your employees. Talk to your **customers**. Run focus groups. Send out surveys. Do hardcore research. Leverage feedback tools with technology, like email, text, and website analytics. The sky is wide open as to how you want to do it. Just get data.

Most importantly, have a conversation *with* (whether it be through technology or face-to-face) and listen *to* whomever you're defining as your "customer." Really. Listen to SERVE.

Fourth, clearly **define** the problem based on your data and the information from the customer. If you don't have it right, start over.

Note: we often get asked the question from our clients, "You said offsite. Does the meeting really have to be?" The answer is no, though you need a space that is both neutral and devoted to being creative – a creative suite, if you will. If you're onsite at your company, people are easily distracted and pulled into conversations. Get away. We promise it will help put people into a different state of mind. Or, spend money on that Innovation Room described later in this section.

Imagine

The third stage in the methodology is to IMAGINE your solution. Bring your **people** together. Do The Improv Mindset exercises and start playing.

Diversify your team in order to get different **perspectives**. Look for people who are involved in the process of creation at all levels. Look for people who aren't involved in the process, as they may surprise you with good ideas.

Most of us surround ourselves with people who think JUST LIKE US. This is called "Confirmation Bias." Think about your friends for a second – we guarantee that most of them think like you do. They agree with your perceptions of things, take the same side in discussions of difficult or polarizing topics, and generally "feel" the way you do about the world. This makes a lot of sense. Why would you surround yourself with conflicting views every day? This would make for a stressful life, yes?

With Confirmation Bias, the more we can surround ourselves with people who think and feel like us, the more we validate our own thinking and beliefs – and that feels good. We are mindful about justifying our views and opinions and actively seek out that support.[68]

It's not just your friends, though – you'll see this in business, as well. Bosses very often hire "in their image," making for a homogenous and consistent team. Great for the status quo...and what happens when you need to think differently?

One of our clients has chosen to deal with the Confirmation Bias by changing their hiring practices. If a candidate makes it all the way to the end of the interview process (which involves several rounds of interviews) and does not get a final selection by the team, a certain percentage of the candidates turned down is *offered the job*. The concept being that there are good reasons that the candidate made it all the way to the end, and

---

[68] (Cooper, 2019)

that there's a high likelihood that Confirmation Bias is coming into play.

It isn't necessary to take team diversification to such an extreme, however. As you're identifying team members for the IMAGINE stage, challenge yourself to look for people who are different from you. They might be in various parts of the organization, or in roles that are completely unrelated to the task. It doesn't matter what level they are.

Once you have **people** and **perspectives** in place, come up with crazy **ideas** for how to solve your problem or challenge. Explore and evaluate your solutions. Talk about them. Play with them.

 ### Idea Prioritization Worksheet

When you're done, take all your solutions, put a value to them, and pick the ones with the most excitement and potential. Rank them using the worksheet in Figure 48.

Instructions for the Idea Prioritization Worksheet:

1) Weight each question based on its importance (1 being the lowest, 10 the highest).

2) Rate the solution against the question (again 1 being the lowest, 10 the highest).

3) Multiply the Weight x Rating to "score" the idea on that particular question.

4) In the case of questions 7-10, the scores are "negative" because the idea may have a large impact on the organization, or there is already a solution that could work.

5) Add up the values in the Score column to get the total score.

Question	Weight (1-10)	Idea #1		Idea #2	
		Rating (1-10)	Score (Weight x Rating)	Rating (1-10)	Score (Weight x Rating
Does the idea get people excited?					
Does the idea contribute value?					
Does the opportunity outweigh the cost?					
How feasible is the idea?					
Is there a way to build a working model without designing the entire thing?					
Does the idea solve everything it needs to?					
Is there a substitute for the idea?			-		-
Can we "buy" the idea? Is there something off-the-shelf that already exists?			-		-
Will we need new infrastructure to support the idea?			-		-
Are there far reaching impacts into other parts of the organization?			-		-
TOTAL					

Figure 48: Idea Prioritization Worksheet

Once you have your total scores, you should have a good sense of which idea might make the most sense to implement. Also, don't be limited by the ten questions we listed above. You might include additional questions that are unique for your organization. For example, if your company is international, there may be a language barrier or another infrastructure question to consider.

Implement

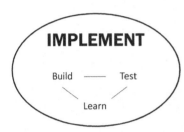

The fourth stage in the methodology is to IMPLEMENT. *Build* something quickly and get it out into the hands of your customer or your employees.

IT DOESN'T HAVE TO BE A COMPLETELY FINISHED PRODUCT.

Don't make the mistake of thinking you need to have everything perfectly designed before you release it.

Just *build* something – anything – with which you can gather feedback. Consider creating things like:

- A picture
- A comic strip
- A cardboard prototype
- A video or movie
- A fake front-end website
- A manual process that emulates all steps

- A role play

Do it. Then go and **test** your solution. Fail and **learn** everything you can. Document that learning and have it influence your design or idea. Then **build** it again.

This part of the process is based around the concept of a minimum viable product (MVP), popularized by Eric Ries in *The Lean Startup*. With this approach, you only develop what is necessary to test your solution and see whether it's workable. Therefore, you limit your overall risk while still getting the valuable data you need.

There are lots of examples where the MVP approach has worked well. For example, the founders of Zappos, the online shoe company, purchased shoes as needed from local retailers, rather than investing in their own inventory. This allowed them to test their business model without investing in additional overhead. The CEO of Dropbox, the online data storage company, created a video that demonstrated how the product would work, without an actual working product. He posted it to HackerNews and overnight they went from 5,000 to 75,000 people on their beta list. The user community went nuts. Flickr, the online photo sharing company, was conceived on a napkin.

The important thing is to get something out into the world so that you can see what works and what doesn't.

Time Boxing

There is a helpful concept to keep in mind as you're working through any one of the pieces of The Improv Mindset 4i Methodology.

How many times have you been in a meeting that spawns four additional meetings because people cannot make a decision? There can be lots of reasons for this – the right people aren't around the table, you don't have all the information, or you can't reach consensus.

We find there's a reason that's a lot more common: people are *afraid* to make a decision. Making a decision means that something will most likely change, and we've talked throughout this book about how the brain reacts to change. There is an additional fear-based reason as well. If a decision **is** made, someone must take responsibility for its potential failure.

People get caught in the "Analysis/Paralysis Cycle," where it's more important to get just a little more information so that the best decision can be made...and then they require a little more information...and then a little more. And then NOTHING GETS DECIDED! We hate that.

We address this challenge through improv by "time boxing" exercises – in business, setting a goal that a decision will be made by a certain time.

All improv exercises have a beginning, a middle, and an end. You know when they start, and you have a good sense of when they're finished. During that time, you are forced to make decisions that move the action forward – decision after decision after decision. You don't have the luxury of sitting back and getting additional information. The additional information comes from YOU!

Researchers at Harvard have determined that enforcing a time limit on a creative effort can produce faster creative thinking...with one caveat: the team must be focused on a mission.[69]

---

[69] (Amabile, Hadley, & Kramer, 2002)

Think of the Apollo 13 ground crew when they had to figure out how to remove the carbon dioxide onboard with extremely limited materials on a badly damaged spacecraft – and then get that spacecraft home! Or the more recent trend of "puzzle rooms" that have grown in popularity in Japan and the U.S. Small groups get locked in a room with puzzles that they must solve in order to get out of the room. They all work on the mission together to escape, and they usually need to complete it in under an hour. Time boxing sets the boundaries needed to move things forward.

It's important not to confuse "time boxing" with "time pressure." Time pressure is that relentless clock at work that is forcing you to complete things by a certain time. "I need that budget by tomorrow." "You'd better get this deployed by Friday or you're fired." "Our customers need this yesterday!"

Time boxing on the other hand, is the process of:

- Identifying a creative challenge clearly and concisely
- Providing a physical space where people can be devoted only to that task
- Giving a hard and fast time limit
- Trusting the decision or solution that emerges

When All Else Fails, Stand Up

T

Stand Up

Have you ever noticed that the typical meeting, brainstorming session or problem-solving workshop begins with everyone *sitting*? Why IS that?

Well, we aren't really sure. Think about it: where do you do your best thinking? Is it sitting in an uncomfortable chair staring blankly into a computer screen or at a blank piece of paper? Our guess is NO. You, like many others, probably get your "aha" moments when showering, driving in your car, exercising, walking, cooking, etc.

A study at Washington University in St. Louis analyzed the group performance of 214 undergraduate students. As part of the study, they divided the students into groups of 3-5 (giving them 54 groups to study). Then they asked each group to complete a creativity task. Half of the groups were directed to a conference room in which there were a table and chairs. The other half had only the table, which forced the team to remain standing. They found that the teams that were standing were not only creative, they were also more collaborative![70]

Even just walking can make a difference. People like Jack Dorsey of Twitter, Steve Jobs of Apple, and Mark Zuckerberg of Facebook swear by the "walking meeting." Researchers at Stanford University found that people were more creative after spending time walking. This makes some sense. Think about what must happen in the brain when you're walking. Various subsystems need to engage – systems that are related to breathing, balance, and pacing. Some researchers suspect that by distracting those parts of the brain, you allow creative thought to come through.[71] Sound familiar?

Does this mean you should have every meeting walking or standing? Probably not. Though, you might want to try changing things up a bit. For example, consider the following:

---

[70] (Knight & Baer, 2014)

[71] (Oppezzo & Schwartz, 2014)

- Try a new space for your meetings – in a coffee shop, in a hallway, or in the kitchen

- Hand out white board pens as people walk into a conference room and force them all to stand

- Take a walk around your office or outside while you talk

- Better yet – go gather in the Innovation Room that's discussed in the next subsection!

Innovation Room

Innovation Room

Take a moment to think back to your childhood. Do you remember what your Kindergarten classroom looked like? It was most likely filled with bright colors and mats on the floor. What creative learning tools did you have access to? Blocks, wood, and multi-colored pens for use on blank pieces of paper.

Now think of your average conference room – what's in there? A table. Chairs. Maybe some inspirational quotes on the walls, if you're lucky. And what tools do you have? Pens. A notebook of lined paper. A laptop and projector...

Guess which one is better for creativity?

Yes, *we all need to return to our Kindergartner roots*.

The Innovation Room is specifically designed space(s) in your offices that you set aside with the sole purpose of inspiring creative thought, supporting brainstorming sessions, stimulating intelligent conversation, and stirring up the hum-drum atmosphere that can pervade workspaces.

If you don't have one, we recommend that you create one as soon as possible.

You should look to your teams to be part of the creation of this environment (and remember to keep the "Yes, and..." approach while doing so). Think of what you want this room to be. Ask the following questions:

- Do you envision easy teaming and collaboration?

- Do you want access to multi-media and digital support?

- Do you want to encourage play? Is it meditative? Both?

You and your teams have a fantastic opportunity to develop a space for all employees to break out of the mundane. It can even change during the day – starting out as one space before work, converting to another space during business hours, and becoming a completely new space at the end of the day. Think of the possibilities!

The following design aspects are ideas for customizing your Innovation Room to get you started. Consider:

- *Lighting:* Warm or cool, bright or dim, or any of the above based on timed settings, your room's lighting source(s) will be a huge factor in determining the feel of the area.

- *Texture/Fabrics/Tactile nature:* Strong lines, metal, plastic, or wood? Soft curves with fabric, pillows, floor seating? Walls that are sound proofed with spongy memory foam? Why not?

- *Colors:* You want to replicate the ocean? How about the mountains? Space? Your choice.

- **Furniture:** From pillows to chairs to overstuffed couches, the possibilities are endless. Red mats for naptime? Treadmills or bouncy balls? A pool table? Pinball machine?

- **Temperature:** Creating a room that is automated to accommodate changes in temperature can be tricky, yet having a space that is uncomfortable and takes you out of your "element" can be counter-productive to the room's intent.

- **View:** Windows or none? Some spaces won't be able to offer a view, and that's fine. Deciding whether it is an important component of your design is something you need to do early on. It's also important to keep in mind that you may not want staff peeking in on folks in the room, so think about shades or etched glass to support privacy.

- **Location:** Keep in mind that the location of this space is very important. If your staff can't easily access it, or it will be disruptive to a typically quiet work area, you might want to rethink it.

- **Games:** There are a truckload of inspiring games out there for this room to house. Silly Putty, Jenga, Legos, Mancala, etc. Invest in them.

- **Music/Sound:** Do you want speakers so that your staff can have a dance party? Or a bunch of Beats headphones so they can escape into their own world and jam? New age music? Nature sounds? Rock or alternative at lunch?

- **Food/Beverages:** Nourishing the body is as important as nourishing the mind. Protein bars, nuts, fruit, juices, teas, coffees. Providing quality treats in this space is a good idea. Think of time lost in offices when staff leave to go to their local coffee shop. We aren't saying you need to chain their ankles to their desks here, just remember that if you build it, they will come.

- ***Reading materials:*** Set aside some space to stack books and magazines you want your staff to have access to while in the Innovation Room. If you are a biomedical engineering firm, it doesn't have to be all medical device mags. The point is to inspire your teams when they are in this room. They probably already know about what's in *Biomedical Engineering Today*. What they need is the book or magazine that's offering ideas about how to think, strategize, create, or become agile and creative. Like, say, ***THIS*** book!

Of course, these are all just ideas – some will work for your company, and some won't. Don't get tricked into thinking you need a massive budget to get it going. Just like the Implement stage in the 4i Methodology, you just need to start with **something.** Start small and grow it when you can.

Make the Innovation Room a priority for your teams. Giving them a space where they can go to be creative can make a huge difference. We promise.

Final Thoughts

"Nothing is stronger than habit."
                                              – Ovid

So, what comes next? How do you take this information and begin building your own individual, team and organizational Improv Mindset?

We mentioned in the Introduction that **The Improv Mindset takes time**. Everyone must learn, understand and play from the same rulebook before you'll truly see any major change. This is not a "read a book and everything will be fine" approach. **You need to practice**. And be committed to the outcome.

There are many things that can influence your ability to create a culture of The Improv Mindset – things like: your organizational design, where you and your company are on the innovation continuum, and how much improvisational collaboration is already occurring.

That said, our recommendation is that **you shouldn't go this alone**. What we've found works best is to:

- Get *everyone* on board and trained with The Improv Mindset

- Do the train-the-trainer approach and designate in-office trainers who become certified to teach The Improv Mindset 4i Methodology to moderate brainstorming sessions and manage on-going training for new employees

- Perform quarterly "tune-ups" for your trainers so that they can stay up to date with new methods and practices

- Perform a culture analysis and find out where gaps are in your various teams

Most importantly, *just get started.*

The Improv Mindset approach *increases communication and listening, creates collaborative and creative teams, unifies employees within a culture and democratizes innovation.* Anyone and everyone will be impacted. Everyone has the potential to change. This powerful breakthrough is just around the corner, as long as you change your mindset – from your brain, to your team, your corporate culture, to your methodology.

With everyone possessing The Improv Mindset, there's no telling *WHAT* radical changes and success you'll experience.

Change your brain. Change your business.

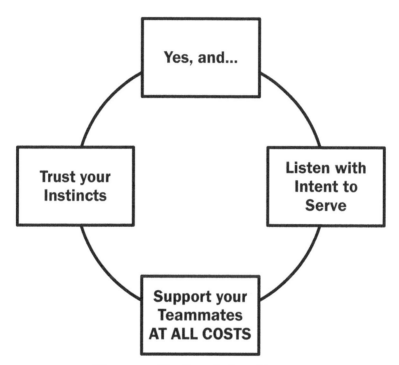

Figure 49: The Four Rules of Improv

Appendix

One Month Improv Mindset Training

You'll be surprised to see your ability to come up with new ideas and make new connections improve dramatically if you commit 5-10 minutes a day for the next thirty days by engaging in the following exercises. As we've outlined throughout this book, ***practicing is key*** in changing neural pathways and significantly altering conditioned brain patterns.

The training is focused on you and your individual creativity, though there's nothing stopping you from doing it as a group (Figure 50). The training consists of several different exercises, all of which are described in detail later in this Appendix. They are:

- Alternate Uses Test (AUT)

- Similar Uses Test (SUT)

- Remote Associates Test (RAT)

- Incomplete Figure Test (IFT)

- Riddles

- Opposite Hand Day (OHD)

- New Designer (ND)

- Build a 3D Face (B3DF)

- Connect the Random (CTR)

- Upside-down Drawing (UD)

For the best results, use the table below as the schedule for the next four weeks. Where appropriate, chart your results from day to day.

	Mon	Tues	Wed	Thurs	Fri
Week 1	AUT	SUT	RAT	IFT	RIDDLE
Week 2	OHD	ND	B3DF	CTR	UD
Week 3	SUT	IFT	AUT	RIDDLE	RAT
Week 4	UD	OHD	CTR	B3DF	ND

Figure 50: Improv Mindset Individual Training Schedule

Exercise 1: Alternate Uses Test (AUT)

Time: approximately 4 minutes

Steps: This exercise is like the exercise we performed at the beginning of this book. Take an everyday object and think of as many different uses for it other than the use of intended design. Example objects could include: business card, stapler, picture frame, scissors, or a computer keyboard.

Here's the first one to get you started (Figure 51). Over the next two minutes think of as many ways that you can use a ***coffee cup*** as possible. Go.

Different Ways to Use a Coffee Cup	
1)	11)
2)	12)
3)	13)
4)	14)
5)	15)
6)	16)
7)	17)
8)	18)
9)	19)
10)	20)

Figure 51: Different Ways to Use a Coffee Cup

Debrief: You will find that some days yield far better results than others. Rate yourself, and list why you think you had the results you did. See if you can identify patterns on good days and bad days. Things to consider include:

- What was your frame of mind when you started?
- Were you hungry or well fed?
- Was there bad traffic?
- Was there noise distracting you?

Exercise 2: Similar Uses Test (SUT)

Time: Approximately 4 minutes

Steps: This exercise is like the AUT in that you're going to use an everyday object from around your office. Pick an object, say a file cabinet. Next, define what the object does and its function. "A file cabinet is designed to hold paper." Now take two minutes and list as many different objects that are designed to do the same thing. You might come up with a briefcase, photocopier, wrapping for a ream of paper, FedEx box, envelope, or Iron Mountain storage.

Note: like the AUT, don't be limited be the size or shape of the object, be creative as to how you define the function of the object. If you picked staple remover, you could define the object as "to remove staples," or as "to pinch at another object to remove something." Which function do you think will get you more creative results?

Take two minutes and use "bookshelf" as your object (Figure 52).

Similar Uses for a Bookshelf	
1)	11)
2)	12)
3)	13)
4)	14)
5)	15)
6)	16)
7)	17)
8)	18)
9)	19)
10)	20)

Figure 52: Similar Uses for a Bookshelf

Debrief: As with the AUT, you will find that some days have far better results than others. Rate yourself, and list why you think you performed the way you did. See if you can identify patterns for both good days and bad days. Things to consider include:

- What was your frame of mind when you started?

- Were you hungry or well fed?

- Was there bad traffic?

- Was there noise distracting you?

Exercise 3: Remote Associates Test (RAT)

Time: approximately 8 minutes

Steps: The Remote Associates Test (RAT) was developed by Sarnoff Mednick in the 1960s as a test used to measure creative thinking. The RAT asks you to come up with the word that links a selection of other words. For example, what connects the following words: Paint / Doll / Cat? The answer: house (house paint, dollhouse, cathouse).

Giving yourself 8 minutes, look at the table below and find the associations – the common word that binds them together (Figure 53). (Answers are at the end of the Appendix)

Items	*Answer*
1) Square / Cardboard / Open	
2) Broken / Clear / Eye	
3) Coin / Quick / Spoon	
4) Time / Hair / Stretch	
5) Land / Hand / House	
6) Hungry / Order / Belt	
7) Way / Ground / Weather	
8) Sore / Shoulder / Sweat	

Figure 53: Remote Associates Test (RAT)

Exercise 4: Incomplete Figure Test

Time: approximately 4 minutes

Steps: This exercise is pure creativity and "out-of-the-box" thinking. One of the most iconic elements of the Torrance Test for Creative Thought (TTCT) is the Incomplete Figure test, a drawing challenge.

1) Give yourself five minutes to see what you can turn them in to. Uncommon subject matter, implied stories, humor, and original perspective all earn high marks.

2) See examples below for your first two challenges (Figure 54). Go here to find other incomplete figures or have someone create a few for you, like your child or co-worker. (We used to play a game with our kids as they were growing up that is exactly like this – we called it the "doodle game" – one person would create a fairly simple doodle and the other person had to make something out of it. As they got older, we applied some rules to it to stretch ourselves such as NO FACES...)

3) Now, giving yourself 5 minutes, look at the figure and open your mind to the possibilities of what it could be. Turn the page around. Envision it as filled in, or a small part of something much bigger.

Note: Many of our clients struggle with this exercise as it's been awhile since they did some serious doodling. Maybe take the first minute to allow for many ideas instead of settling on the first instinct. You may find yourself eventually going back to that idea as the final decision, and that's totally fine. It's just a good idea to not lock yourself in too early. Think of the possibilities!

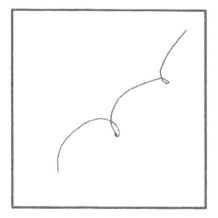

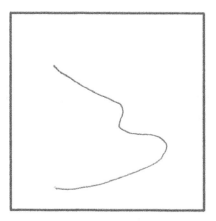

Figure 54: Incomplete Figure Test

See the Answers section toward the end of the book for an example of a completed test.

Exercise 5: Riddles

Time: approximately 5 minutes

Steps: You may remember reading Tolkien novels or playing around with riddles when you were younger. Here's one we remember from *"The Hobbit."*

> A box without hinges, key or lid,
>
> Yet golden treasure inside is hid.

Answer: Egg

Now here's one for you. Take up to 10 minutes to answer the following riddle. Remember to allow yourself to stay open minded and avoid locking in or forcing an answer to fit. Of course, if you're able to solve it quickly, that's great! Also, don't beat yourself up if you struggle to identify it right away – the point is to give your brain that much needed daily workout.

- *Question:* We hurt without moving. We poison without touching. We bear the truth and the lies. We are not to be judged by our size. What are we? (the answer is on the last few pages of the book)

You can find more riddles at the following websites:

- www.goodriddlesnow.com
- www.riddlers.org
- http://www.buzzle.com/articles/hard-riddles-for-adults.html

Exercise 6: Opposite Hand Day (OHD)

**Time:** As much as you can all day

**Steps:** This exercise is focused on breaking existing habitual patterns, and naturally forcing you into being truly present. If you're like most people in the world you have a dominant hand, and you use that dominant hand for most of your day. The challenge: take everyday tasks and attempt to do them with the opposite hand.

Be creative in identifying your tasks that you'll practice. You include things like:

- Washing your hair or your body
- Answering the phone (including which pocket you keep it in)
- Buttoning your shirt or pants
- Combing your hair
- Unlocking the car
- Using your credit card

The goal is: wherever you can use your non-dominant hand, give it a try.

Exercise 7: New Designer (ND)

Time: Approximately 10 minutes

Steps: This exercise is focused on getting your brain into a different mindset when it looks at commonplace items.

1) Identify an item in your office. It can be anything – a laptop, a desk lamp, or an HDMI cable, for example.

2) Identify three different designers or companies that are now going to redesign that item. For example, General Motors, Oprah Winfrey, and NASA.

3) With your item in mind, spend three minutes coming up with ideas on a piece of paper that lists features of the item if your first designer/company was to design it. Think about things like what material would be used, what would adorn it, what other functions can be added to it.

4) Don't judge your ideas. Just get them down on paper.

Example:

Let's say that our item is a coffee cup and that we will use the two of the designers/companies we listed above (General Motors and NASA).

General Motors

- Chrome handle

- Little mini-motor and four wheels that allows the coffee to drive around and be delivered

- Engine sounds every time you drink

- 3D coffee cup hood ornament on the bottom

- Convertible top that allows the coffee to stay warm, and it folds out LIKE a convertible
- Brake lights when the coffee gets low

NASA

- Titanium cup
- Anti-gravity spill prevention
- Made of moon rocks
- Hovers off the ground
- If you want to save your coffee it allows you to freeze dry it and reconstitute it later
- Designed to look like the lunar rover; the handle is Neil Armstrong climbing down the ladder.

As you can see, these ideas are WAY out there, and we haven't limited our imagination. We had fun identifying the crazy things that could be added. Think if there was actually anti-gravity spill prevention. We'd get behind that tomorrow!

Exercise 8: Build a 3D Face

Time: 5 minutes

Steps: This exercise takes objects that you have around you and forces you to build a 3D face in front of you.

Grab any and all items around you and get to work. You are trying to build a face as if it's looking right at you. Try not to just draw things – No points if you draw eyes and a mouth, for example. The whole point is to think differently and create something out of seemingly random items (i.e., pens, stapler, shredded paper, paperclips, phone, etc.).

Exercise 9: Connect the Random (CTR)

Time: Approximately 7 minutes

Steps: The purpose of this exercise is to force connections between items that would not normally be associated together. Start by thinking of 5 items in your refrigerator.

Now think of 5 items in your boiler room.

You might have two lists that look like this (Figure 55):

Refrigerator	Boiler Room
Eggs	Screwdriver
Orange juice	Hot water heater
Left over pizza	Copper tubing
Olives	Power drill
White wine	Paint can

Figure 55: List of Items

Now think of three professions – for example, you might have astronaut, or race car driver, or surfer.

As quickly as you can, combine one word from each of the lists, then name and describe a product for one of the professions. For example (Figure 56):

Profession	Product	Description
Astronaut	Copper tubing eggs	A product that spawns additional copper tubing

		when needed in space. It basically grows copper in case of an emergency.
Race car driver	Power drill ol-ives	A product used for staying fed while working on the car. Anytime you need a snack, the power drill pro-duces olives to stave off hunger.
Surfer	Orange Juice Paint Can	Everyone knows that surf-ers need to be able to stick to their boards. This is a completely eco-friendly alternative to wax so that your surfer can hang ten with confidence. Just spread the Orange Juice Paint over the board and you're good to go.

Figure 56: Connect the Random Example

Exercise 10: Upside Down Drawing

Time: Approximately 10 minutes

Steps: The purpose of this exercise is to change your perspective so that it's easier draw something.

Let's start with a question: If we were to ask you whether or not you could draw, most of you would answer "no." Yet, if we were to ask the same question of a group of Kindergartners, every one of them would scream, "Yes!".

Why is that? Likely we've added a bunch of our own self-criticism about how we think things need to look. Let's let go of that for now.

Open your smartphone and navigate to your Photos app. Pick one of the images and spend 5 minutes drawing it. How'd you do? Not impressed?

Now turn your phone upside down and spend 5 minutes drawing it again (note: you may have to configure the rotation setting on the phone so that the picture can stay upside down).

Compare the two images. Is one better than the other? We often find with our clients that the second image is easier to draw and as a result the "better" image. Why do you think that is? We believe that we are not so locked into what the "right" image must be when it's upside down. Paradoxically, we see the image more clearly when it's facing a different direction.

The point is this: a simple shift in perspective can make all the difference when it comes to flexing our creative muscles.

Answers

Remote Associates Test (RAT) – Answers

Items	Answer
1) Square / Cardboard / Open	Box
2) Broken / Clear / Eye	Glass
3) Coin / Quick / Spoon	Silver
4) Time / Hair / Stretch	Long
5) Land / Hand / House	Farm
6) Hungry / Order / Belt	Money
7) Way / Ground / Weather	Fair
8) Sore / Shoulder / Sweat	Cold

Figure 57: Remote Associates Test (RAT) – Answers

Riddle

Words.

Here's an example of what you might have come up with for the Incomplete Figure Test (Figure 58).

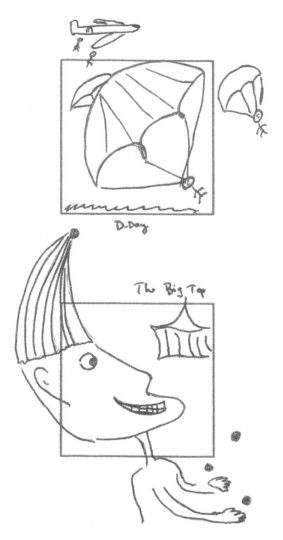

Figure 58: Incomplete Figure Test (example)

References

Alia-Klein, N., Goldstein, R. Z., Tomasi, D., Zhang, L., Fagin-Jones, S., Telangm, F., . . . Volkow, N. D. (2007, August 7). *What is in a Word? No versus Yes Differentially Engage the Lateral Orbitofrontal Cortex.* Retrieved December 12, 2019, from http://www.ncbi.nlm.nih.gov/pmc/articles/PMC2443710/

Amabile, T., Hadley, C. N., & Kramer, S. J. (2002, August 1). *Creativity Under the Gun.* Retrieved December 12, 2019, from https://hbr.org/2002/08/creativity-under-the-gun/ar/1

Andersson, T., Caker, M., Tengblad, S., & Wicklegren, M. (2019). Building traits for organization resilience through balancing organization structures. *Scandinavian Journal of Management*, 36-45.

Arashad, D., Zakaria, N., Kadzrina, A.-K., & Ahmad, N. (2018). Linkage between Flexibility and SMEs Performance: Does Improvisation Matter? *MATEC Web of Converences.*

Auletta, K. (2014, February 3). *Outside the Box.* Retrieved December 12, 2019, from http://www.newyorker.com/magazine/2014/02/03/outside-the-box-2

Barret, K. C., & Limb, C. J. (2020). Functional Magnetic Resonance Imaging (fMRI) and the Neural Correlates of Artistic Creative Production. *Encyclopedia of Creativity.*

Baumann, O., & Stieglitz, N. (2014). Rewarding Value-Creating Ideas in Organizations: The Power of Low-Powered Incentives. *Strategic Management Journal, 35*(3), 358-375.

Bechtoldt, M. (2017, July 26). *Emotional Intelligence.* Retrieved from
      Oxford Bibliographies:
      https://www.oxfordbibliographies.com/view/document/obo-
      9780199846740/obo-9780199846740-0130.xml

Brain Clinics. (2016, February 8). *Dorsolateral Prefrontal Cortex (Brain
      Clinics).* Retrieved from Brain Clinics:
      http://www.brainclinics.com/dynamic/media/1/images/rTMS/D
      LPFC_Left.jpg

Brown, S. E. (1998). *Competing on the Edge - Strategy as Structured
      Chaos.* Boston, MA: Harvard Business Press.

Buck, R. (2008, April 30). *The Funny Business of Laughter.* Retrieved from
      http://www.sciencefocus.com/feature/psychology/funny-
      business-laughter

Capodagli, B., & Jackson, L. (2010). Collaboration in the Sandbox. In
      Innovate the Pixar Way (pp. 62-65). New York: McGraw Hill.

Caruana, F. (2017). Laughter as a Neurochemical Mechanism Aimed at
      Reinforcing Social Bonds: Integrating Evidence from Opiodergic
      Activity and Brain Stimulation. *The Journal of Neuroscience,*
      8581-8582.

Cooper, B. B. (2019, 12 11). *blog.bufferapp.com.* Retrieved from Bufferapp:
      https://blog.bufferapp.com/thinking-mistakes-8-common-
      mistakes-in-how-we-think-and-how-to-avoid-them

Coulson-Thomas, C. (2017). Corporate Leadership for an Uncertain and
      Cynical Age. *Effective Executive,* 15-30.

Favara Jr., L. (2009, April 1). *Examining Followership Styles and Their
      Relationship with Job Satisfaction and Performance.* Retrieved
      from http://pqdtopen.proquest.com/doc/305167384
      .html?FMT=ABS

Forrester Research. (2014). *The Creative Dividend: How Creativity Impacts Business Results*. Cambridge: Forrester Research.

Golis, C. (2013, January 01). *A Brief History of Emotional Intelligence*. Retrieved from Practical Emotional Intelligence: https://www.emotionalintelligencecourse.com/history-of-eq/

Goodall, W. (2015, February 18). *Watchmen Blog*. Retrieved December 12, 2019, from northwestu.edu: https://www.northwestu.edu/watchmen/developing-healthy-relationships-by-listening/

Gopalkrishnan, S. (2017). The Role of Humor in Startup Success: The Mediating Role of Team Performance. *Journal of Organizational Psychology*.

Guittierez, G. (2014, November 17). *Are Corporations People Too?* Retrieved December 2, 2014, from https://www.bcm.edu/news/neuroscience/are-corporations-people-too

Gutman, R. (2011, May 11). *The Hidden Power of Smiling - Transcript*. (TED) Retrieved from http://www.ted.com/talks/ron_gutman_the_hidden_power_of_smiling/transcript?language=en

Hamzeh, F. R., Alhussein, H., & Faek, F. (2018). Investigating the Practice of Improvisation in Construction. *Journal of Management in Engineering*.

Hassan, K. (2019, January 20). Creativity Trilateral Dynamics: Playfulness, Mindfulness, and Improvisation. *Creativity Studies*, 1-14.

Hill, K. E., Bush, V. D., Vorhies, D., & King, R. A. (2017). Performing Under Pressure: Winning Customers Through Improvisation in Team Selling. *Journal of Relationship Marketing*, 227-244.

Jr., L. F. (2009). *Examining Followership Styles and Their Relationship with Job Satisfaction and Performance*. Ann Arbor: ProgQuest LLC.

Kelley, R. E. (1992). *The Power of Followership: How to create leaders people want to follow and followers who lead themselves.* New York: Currency/Doubleday.

Kempe, M., & Memmert, D. (2018, April 6). "Good, better, creative": the influence of creativity on goal scoring in elite soccer . *Journal of Sports Sciences*, pp. 2419-2423.

Knight, A. P., & Baer, M. (2014, November 1). Get Up, Stand Up: The Effects of a Non-Sedentary Workspace on Information Elaboration and Group Performance. *Social Psychological and Personality Science,* 5(8), 910-917.

Kocak, G. (2018). The Relationship Between Humor Styles and Creativity: A Research on Academics. *Eurasian Journal of Business Management*, 44-58.

Kudrowitz, B. (2010, September 10). HaHa and Aha! Creativity, Idea Generation, Improvisational Humor, and Product Design. Boston, MA, USA.

Land, G., & Jarman, B. (1992). *Breakpoint and Beyond: Mastering the Future Today.* New York: HarperBusiness.

Law, K., W. C., & Song, L. (2004). The construct and criterion validity of emotional intelligence and its potential utility for management studies. *Journal of Applied Psychology*, 483-496.

Leadum, R. (2018, 08 12). *Why Emotional Intelligence Is Crucial for Success (Infographic).* Retrieved from Entrepreneur: https://www.entrepreneur.com/article/318187

Lehmann-Willenbrock, N., & Allen, J. A. (2014). How Fun Are Your Meetings? Investigating the Relationship Between Humor Patterns in Team Interactions and Team Performance. *Journal of Applied Psychology, 99(6), 1278-1287.*

Liu, S., Chow, H. M., Yisheng Xu, M. G., Swett, K. E., Eagle, M. W., Rizik-Baer, D. A., & Braun, A. R. (2012, November 15). *Neural Correlates of Lyrical Improvisation: An fMRI Study of Freestyle Rap*. Retrieved from http://www.nature.com/srep/2012/121115/srep00834/full/srep00834.html

Liu, Y., Diwei, L., Ying, Y., Arndt, F., & Wei, J. (2018). Improvisation for innovation: The contingent role of resource and structural factors in explaining innovation capability. *Technovation*, 32-41.

Lopata, J., Nowicki, E., & Joanisse, M. (2017). Creativity as a distinct trainable mental state: An EEG study of musical improvisation. *Neuropsycholgia*, 246-258.

Magni, M., & Palmi, P. S. (2017). Under Pressure! Team innovative climate and individual attitudes in shaping individual improvisation. *European Management Journal*, 474-484.

Maimone, F., & Sinclair, M. (2014). Dancing in the dark: creativity knowledge creation and (emergent) organizational change. *Journal of Organizational Change Management*, 344-361.

Manninnen, S., Tuonminen, L., Dunbar, R., Karjalainen, T., Hirvonen, J., Arponen, E., . . . Nummenmaa, L. (2017). Social laughter triggers endogenous opioid release in humans. *Journal of Neuroscience*, 6125-6131.

McCallum, J. S. (2013, September 1). *Followership: The Other Side of Leadership*. Retrieved from http://iveybusinessjournal.com/topics/leadership/followership-the-other-side-of-leadership#.VNZVdy5WJUl

McKeown, M. (2014). The Innovator's Toolkit. In *The Innovation Book* (pp. 52-242). Harlowe, England: Pearson.

Merzenich, M. (2013, August 6). *How You Can Make Your Brain Smarter Every Day*. Retrieved from

http://www.forbes.com/sites/nextavenue/2013/08/06/how-you-
can-make-your-brain-smarter-every-day/

Moran, G. (2014, April 4). *A Real Life Mad Man on Fighting Fear for
Greater Creativity.* Retrieved from fastcompany.com:
http://www.fastcompany.com/3028594/bottom-line/a-real-life-
mad-man-on-fighting-fear-for-greater-creativity

National Institute of Health. (2012, 3 29). *Brain Wiring a No-Brainer.*
Retrieved from http://www.nih.gov/news/health/mar2012/nimh-
29.htm

Nelissen, J. M. (2013). Intuition and Problem Solving. *Curriculum and
Teaching, 28*(2), 27-44.

Nisula, A.-M., & Kianto, A. (2018). Stimulating organisational creativity
with theatrical improvisation. *Journal of Business Research*, 484-
493.

O'Neill, B. (2016). What is the state of play? *International Journal of Play*,
119-122.

Oppezzo, M., & Schwartz, D. L. (2014). Give Your Ideas Some Legs: The
Positive Effect of Walking on Creative Thinking. *Journal of
Experimental Psychology, 40*(4), 1142-1152.

Pentland, A. (2012). The New Science of Building Great Teams. *Harvard
Business Review*(April 2012).

Plitt, M., Savjani, R., Savjani, R., & Eagleman, D. (2015). Are corporations
people too? The neural correlates of moral judgments about
companies and individuals. *Social Neuroscience, 10*(1).

PriceWaterhouseCoopers. (2013, January 1). *Breakthrough Innovation and
Growth.* Retrieved from http://download.pwc.com/ie/pubs/
2013_breakthrough_innovation_and_growth.pdf

Pysch-It. (2015, July 4). *Dorsolateral Prefontal Cortex*. (Psych-It) Retrieved January 10, 2015, from Psych-It: http://www.psych-it.com.au/Psychlopedia/article.asp?id=191

Richard, V., Halliwell, W., & Tenenbaum, G. (2017). Effects of a Improvisation Intervention on Elite Figure Skaters' Performance, Self Esteem, Creativity, and Mindfulness Skills. *The Sports Pyschologist*, 275-287.

Robinson, K. (2010, Oct 14). *RSA Changing Education Paradigms*. (RSA) Retrieved from https://www.youtube.com/watch?v= zDZFcDGpL4U

RSA. (2010, October 14). *RSA Animate - Changing Paradigms*. (RSA Animate) Retrieved January 29, 2015, from http://www.thersa.org/events/rsaanimate/animate/rsa-animate-changing-paradigms

Salopek, J. (1991, September 1). Is Anyone Listening? *Training & Development*.

Samani, M., & Thomas, R. (2017, January 11). Your Leadership Development Program Needs an Overhaul. *HRNews; Alexandria*, 1-4.

Sawyer, K. (2007). Group Genius. In *Improvising Innovation* (p. 28). New York: Basic Books.

Sharma, A., & Bhatnagar, J. (2017). Emergence of team engagement under time pressure: role of team leader and team climate. *Team Performance Management*, 171-185.

Sowden, P., Clements, L., Redlich, C., & Lewis, C. (2015). Improvisation facilitates divergent thinking and creativity: Realizing a benefit of primary school arts education. *Psychology of Aesthetics, Creativity, and the Arts*, 128-138.

Sundheim, D. (2013, January 9). *To Increase Innovation, Take the Sting Out of Failure*. Retrieved from https://hbr.org/2013/01/to-increase-innovation-take-th/

the-numbers.com. (2020, January 1). *Box Office History for Disney-Pixar Movies*. (Nash Information Services, LLC) Retrieved January 1, 2020, from https://www.the-numbers.com/movies/production-company/Pixar

Trepanier, S., & Nordgren, M. (2017). Improvisation for Leadership Development. *The Journal of Continuing Education in Nursing*, 151-153.

Trotter, M., Salmon, P., Goode, N., & Lenne, M. (2018). Distributed improvisation: a systems perspective of improvisation 'epics' by led outdoor activity leaders. *Ergonomics*, 295-312.

Tuckman, B. W. (1965). Development Sequence in Small Groups. *Psychological Bulletin, 63*(6), 384-399.

VanDerveer, B., & Butterick, B. (2016, November/December). Championship Communication. *Strategies, 30*, 5-9.

Vestberg, T., Gustason, R. M., & Petrovic, P. (2012). Executive Functions Predict the Success of Top-Soccer Players. *PLoS One*, 7(4): e34731.

Walker, C. J. (2010). Experiencing flow: Is doing it together better than doing it alone? *The Journal of Positive Pyschology*, 3-11.

WD-40. (2014, 12 29). *Fascinating Facts You Never Learned in School*. (WD-40) Retrieved from http://wd40.com/cool-stuff/history

Westbrook, P. (2016, October 16). *Your Brain on Improv*. Retrieved from flutejournal.com: http://flutejournal.com/your-brain-on-improv/

Wikipedia. (2015, January 26). *Agile Software Development*. (Wikipedia) Retrieved from http://en.wikipedia.org/wiki/Agile_software_development

ABOUT THE AUTHORS

Bruce and Gail started ExperienceYes in 2013 and have been quickly building their client base in the fields of telecom, education, oil & gas, healthcare, and management consulting. They both still nurture their passion for performing staying busy with local theatre companies, such as The Evergreen Players and the Evergreen Players improv Comedy troupe (EPiC).

They are married, have two kids, and live in Evergreen, CO. They love to travel internationally to discover great food and new wines.

You can find out more about them and their work on their website https://www.ExperienceYes.com, on LinkedIn, or on Facebook at facebook.com/ExperienceYes.